MUS-BOOK

MT
948
.B72
1982

Bramscher, Cynthia
S., 1948—

Holiday music
activities for the
entire school year

DATE			

Holiday Music
Activities
for the
Entire School Year

Also by the Author

Treasury of Musical Motivators for the Elementary Classroom

Holiday Music Activities for the Entire School Year

Cynthia S. Bramscher

PARKER PUBLISHING COMPANY, INC.
WEST NYACK, NEW YORK

©1982 by

PARKER PUBLISHING COMPANY, INC.
West Nyack, NY

Library of Congress Cataloging in Publication Data

Bramscher, Cynthia S.
　　Holiday music activities for the entire school
year.

　　Bibliography: p.
　　1. Games with music.　2. Musico-calisthenics.
I. Title
MT948.B72　　372.8'7044　　82-6414
　　　　　　　　　　　　　　　AACR2

ISBN 0-13-392613-3

A Word from the Author

If you've ever wondered how you could add an extra sparkle to your students' holiday celebrations, or if you have merely considered ways in which you might break the monotony of the everyday classroom routine with a different type of activity, then *Holiday Music Activities for the Entire School Year* is for you. This book provides practical lesson plans for using music either to enhance those annual holiday events or simply to enliven the daily goings-on in the classroom—musical lesson plans that you can confidently use with the students *regardless of your own musical training or experience*. Whether you require an activity or two to occupy your restless class after the cards have been opened and the treats have been gobbled up at the class Valentine's Day party or if your lethargic students need a "holiday lift" on a long, rainy Friday afternoon, all the lesson plans you will need for revitalizing your youngsters are included in the pages of this handbook.

Here is a practical guide to the successful use of music to add a refreshing new dimension to the traditional classroom holiday observances as well as to brighten the day-to-day academic proceedings. Not dealing in educational theories or philosophies, this book is a collection of innovative, *practical* lesson plans for utilizing various kinds of musical activities to enrich the entire classroom experience. Each plan is explained completely and concisely, using a format of numbered steps. The specific objective of every lesson is given, in addition to suggested grade levels. Thus, the busy classroom teacher may see at a glance the purpose and scope of each activity, game, or project.

Furthermore, each and every lesson plan is designed for immediate use by *any* elementary school teacher, whether musically knowledgeable or not. No technical, complicated musical terminology is used in the book, and any terms that do require explanation are defined on the same page in clear, simple language. Thus, secure in your ability to present these unique and exciting activities to your class, you may fully enjoy the musical encounters along with your students.

Naturally, some preparation on the part of the teacher will be required before conducting a number of the activities, projects, and games with the students. For example, it may be necessary to visit the public library or your district's curriculum center to locate and borrow the various recordings suggested for certain lessons. As for special supplies and materials, none of the lesson plans call for the purchase of expensive equipment to implement the activities. As a matter of fact, the creative use of readily available classroom materials is a recurring theme throughout the book, whether the ideas are originated by the teacher or initiated by the students.

Many of the lesson plans in the book are interchangeable—i.e., a specific plan suggested for use with a certain holiday may be easily adapted to another celebration. In other words, if you happen to be in search of a novel musical game or project for your class's Halloween preparations, don't limit your reading to the chapter centered around that particular holiday theme and forget about the rest of the book. Each of the lesson plans is designed for smooth adaptation to nearly all the traditional holiday observances as well as for invigorating the ordinary workings of the elementary classroom. You need only carefully read each plan, thoroughly familiarize yourself with the material, and let your own teaching instincts and style take over. Should you want a catchy idea for a colorful holiday bulletin board or a rousing team game for recharging your sleepy third graders after lunch hour, you'll find dozens of ready-to-use musical lesson plans to accommodate your every "holiday need."

As mentioned above, various recordings are required for some of the activities, and individual musical examples have been suggested. You might, however, have a different musical composition in mind for a particular activity, and as long as that composition fulfills the need and is appropriate to the chosen activity, go right ahead and use it. Since this book is purposely written to be musically non-technical, all of the recordings listed (with the exception of those cited in lessons requiring specific compositions) may be replaced with recordings of similar musical style or subject. Once again, utilizing the materials and equipment on hand makes these lesson plans extremely attractive to the classroom teacher who has neither the funds nor the inclination to purchase expensive records and tapes. In any event, *all* recordings should be listened to by the teacher before any activity necessitating musical accompaniment is presented to the students.

Regardless of your choice of musical activities to augment your holiday preparations or to highlight the business of the regular classroom day, all of the lesson plans are not only highly stimulating in themselves, but they also encourage the learning of music fundamentals and skills in an animated atmosphere of fun. They vividly demonstrate the very natural relationship of music and those special occasions we call holidays. If to commemorate a particular festive event by illustrating the noisy "Firecrackers" or to celebrate the holiday spirit with a rollicking "Christmas Stocking Relay," all the motivational tools you will need for evoking your students' enthusiastic musical participation in the holiday happenings are presented in the following chapters. Whether interpreting the holiday theme through the creative pantomime of "Little People Predicaments" or by fashioning the delightful "Musical Easter Bonnets," a few minutes set aside for musical activity in the classroom will be welcomed most eagerly by the students.

Above all, you, the elementary classroom teacher, may feel totally capable of leading your students in these richly rewarding holiday musical adventures. Experiment with any or all of the activities, games, and projects, and improvise upon the lesson plans if you wish, modifying the material to your individual needs and to suit your own teaching style and goals. Having prepared yourself completely by carefully reading each step of your chosen activities and thoughtfully planning your presentations to the students, take a positive, active role in the lessons, and savor those musical moments with the kids. The holiday spirit is inherent in virtually all musical expression, and with the assistance of these practical lesson plans both you and your class may experience that holiday feeling every day of the school year.

Cynthia S. Bramscher

SPECIAL THANKS
TO

Dennis Meisinger
The Leonard Winter Family
and
Sybil Grace

Contents

Chapter 6

VALENTINE'S DAY – 103

February 14

Chapter 7

ST. PATRICK'S DAY – 121

March 17

Chapter 8

EASTER – 133

First Sunday after the first full moon following the vernal equinox

Chapter 9

PATRIOTIC HOLIDAYS OF THE SCHOOL YEAR – 153

Veteran's Day – November 11
Lincoln's Birthday – February 12
Washington's Birthday – February 22
Memorial Day – May 30

Holiday Music
Activities
for the
Entire School Year

1

SUMMER HOLIDAY MEMORIES

Independence Day - July 4
Labor Day - First Monday in September

"What did you do on your summer vacation?"

How many times have you asked your class that very question to "break the ice" on the first day back to school in September? How many times have you had to resort to the "old standby" assignments for encouraging your students to share their summertime memories? Jennifer writes a paragraph describing her trip to St. Louis to visit a cousin; Andy draws a picture of the cabin he shared with his dad at the lake; Laurie prepares an oral report on her family's stay at Disneyworld; and so on.

If these routine methods for stimulating student communication on that first day of the fall semester have become a chore for both you and your class, it's time to consider a different way of asking that standard back-to-school question. By combining the magic of two elements—holidays and music—you can successfully implement a new approach for achieving enthusiastic student involvement in relating those enjoyable summer happenings that are common to most young people. Presented in the pages of this chapter is a group of exciting, innovative musical activities designed to motivate your students to creatively express their pleasant remembrances of warm weather and families being together.

Independence Day, for example, is a splendid holiday for introducing music into the beginning-of-the-year classroom proceedings. "Firecrackers," a delightfully noisy activity, offers the students an excellent opportunity to recall and reproduce the distinctive sounds of the Fourth of July fireworks display. The midsummer family outing to the zoo is featured in the charming "Thumbprint Critter Photo Follies," a project for stimulating the students to visually express their interpretations of various musical compositions. "Musical Postcards," an exercise in shaping and sharpening the skill of music listening, prompts the students to reminisce about their favorite vacation locales. Summertime sports—perfect events for blending rhythm and pantomime—are highlighted in such July Fourth activities as "Rhythm Baseball" and "Sports Show." What youngster can resist the attraction and thrills of the amusement park? The visitor to "Boogie Island" is no exception as he romps through the fascinating carnival setting while learning an entire vocabulary of musical words, phrases, and symbols.

Labor Day—the final fling of summer—is a good holiday for enhancing the students' awareness of each other as well as expanding their recognition and appreciation of various jobs, careers, and professions. " 'Getting to Know You' Rhythm Circle" is a prime example—a catchy rhythmic activity by which the students quickly become acquainted with one another. Familiar job symbols are correlated with common musical symbols in "On the Job," and "When I Grow Up" sets the stage for the students to reveal their individual dreams and ambitions through interpretative movement.

Thus, the unique combination of music and summer holiday memories can be a valuable motivational tool for promoting student participation in those all-important first days of the new school year. The elementary classroom is an educational clearing house for the encounter and exchange of thoughts, ideas, and personalities. Creative musical responses to the question "What did you do on your summer vacation?" will establish friendly, open lines of communication and set a positive tone for the remainder of the year to come.

FIRECRACKERS
Bulletin Board Idea

Objective: To develop the ability to represent various sounds visually.

Grades: 3–6

1. Prepare for this activity by covering the bulletin board with plain background paper.
2. Give each student crayons and/or colored pencils.
3. Ask the students to describe or name the various sounds produced by fireworks at Fourth of July celebrations; list these sound words (either legitimate words or those contrived by the students) on the chalkboard:

Whoosh	Crack
Pop	Kaboom
Bang	Sizzle
Fizz	Hiss
Swish	Phhhhht
Boom	Eeeeeee
Whiz	Sssssss

4. Tell the students that each of them is to select one or more words from the above list or invent a fireworks sound word(s) of his own. In groups of two or three at a time, invite the students to draw their words on the bulletin board in such a way as to visually depict the "movement of sound" in a fireworks display:

Note: This particular activity may become a bit noisy at times since the students may find it necessary to vocalize their sound words in order to properly illustrate them on the bulletin board.

BOOGIE ISLAND

Game

Objective: To develop an awareness of common musical symbols and their respective functions and to recognize various musical words and phrases.

Grades: 4–6 (two–four players)

1. You (or a selected student) enlarge the game playing field on page 21 on a large sheet of oaktag, posterboard, or drawing paper:

2. Gather together the following items to be used in playing the game:

   A. One die [1]

   B. Two to four different-colored game markers to be used for movement around the board, such as golf tees, buttons, cardboard or plastic discs, or similar objects

3. Tell the students how to play the game as follows:

   A. The object of the game is to be the first player to complete a trip down the path of the mythical amusement park, Boogie Island, successfully arriving at *Fine*.

   B. Having positioned their markers in the starting zone, the players are ready to roll the die and begin the game. When a player "lands on" a particular space (rectangular or circular) of the path he is to proceed accordingly:

Space on the Path	Procedure
A ride or attraction designated by the symbol ⌒	Lose one turn. (The player takes time out for a ride or attraction.)
♯	Change direction by taking the path to the *right*.
	Change direction by taking the path to the *left*.

---

[1] If commercially made dice are not available, fashion them from styrofoam chunks or block erasers cut into cubes and punctured with small holes to simulate dots.

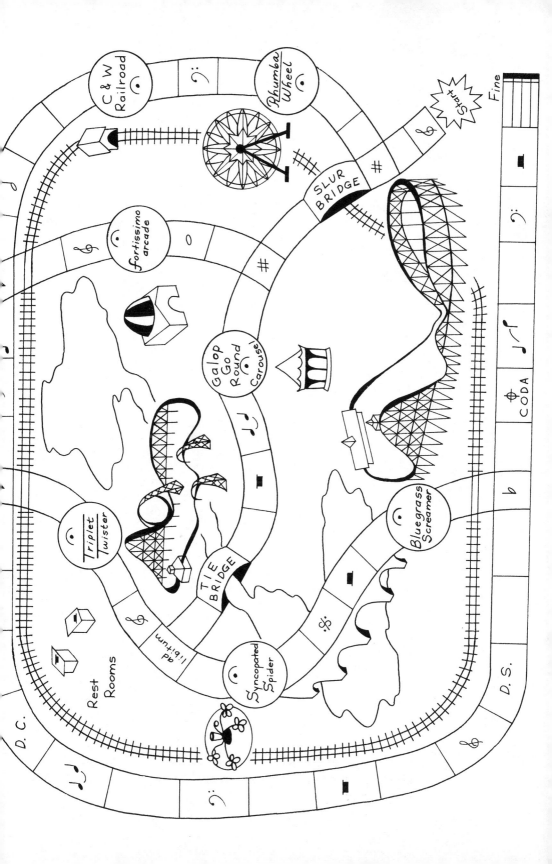

ad libitum

Take the path *either* to the right or the left—at the discretion of the player.

D. C.

Go back to the space labeled START and begin the game over.

D. S.

Go back to the space labeled 𝄋 and proceed from that point.

al 𝄌 Coda

Move directly to the space labeled 𝄌 and proceed CODA from that point.

𝅗𝅥 𝅘𝅥

Move ahead *two* spaces.

𝅘𝅥 𝅘𝅥

Move ahead *four* spaces.

▆

Move off the path to the ▆ rest room and remain there until a "four" is rolled on the die. (The player then places his marker on the space labeled 𝅝 to resume play from that point.)

▆

Move off the path to the ▆ rest room and remain there until a "two" is rolled on the die. (The player then places his marker on the space labeled 𝅗𝅥 to resume play from that point.)

TIE Bridge ⎫
SLUR Bridge ⎭

Slide ahead *one* space.

𝄞 ⎫
𝄢 ⎭

Exchange places with any other player on the board.

C. Unless he lands on a space labeled ♯ or ♭ the player is to continue in a *forward* direction along the path for the duration of the game.

D. It is mandatory that the player who lands on a space labeled 𝄞
or 𝄢 exchange places with another player, no matter how close
to *Fine* that player may be.

4. Depending on the degree of complexity or variety desired, the
game board may be designed to include additional attractions,
each named using a musical word.[2] For example:

Pizzicato Picnic Grounds
Gondola Shuffle (sky ride)
Presto Pizza Stand
Funky Fugue Flume (water flume ride)
Dixieland Jazz Jets
Toccata Turnpike (raceway)
Wild Bongos Fun House
Glissando's Gift Shop
Tempo Tickler (scrambler ride)
Calypso Jungle Cruise
Disco Dodgems (bumper cars)
Staccato Snack Bar
Crescendo Super Slide
Ragtime Rascal (small roller coaster)
Tambourine Twin Spin (double Ferris wheel)

5. In addition, drawing trees and shrubbery on the board will lend
an attractive, landscaped appearance to the park, and the musical
character of the game will be enhanced by naming the various
bodies of water on the playing field. For example, the area of
water surrounding the island may be labeled "Swan Lake," and
the ponds within the park may be designated "Legato Lagoon,"
"Serenade Swamp," or "Piccolo Pond."

6. If desired, this particular game may be adapted for large scale use
within the classroom by drawing the playing field on a large
bedsheet or vinyl floor mat and constructing a very large die from
a square box painted with dots; the students may then actually
walk through their musical amusement park, adding to the fun
and adventure of Boogie Island.

---

[2] On the sample game board illustrated in Step 1, C & W is the abbreviated title of
the Country-Western Railroad.

RHYTHM BASEBALL
Game

Objective: To develop the ability to accurately reproduce a given pattern of rhythmic gestures.

Grades: 1–5 (entire class participation)

1. Explain that the following activity will be a team game, and choose two teams.
2. Each team selects a captain who organizes his members into a "batting order."
3. Tell the students how to play the game as follows:
   A. Each corner of the classroom is designated as a particular "base," and the winning team is the one that earns the most "runs." A run is scored when a team member makes a complete trip around all four bases.
   B. To begin, the first "batter" of the team chosen to start the game walks to the corner of the room selected as "home plate" and stands facing the "pitcher" (the teacher) who stands in the center of the classroom.
   C. You then "pitch" a particular rhythmic sequence to the batter; for example, you may clap your hands together twice and then slap your lap four times in a *definite, steady rhythm.*
   D. The batter must accurately reproduce your pattern of rhythmic movements, *maintaining the established beat,* in order to advance to the corner of the room designated as "first base." (As each batter successfully performs his rhythmic pattern and moves to first base, those players already on other bases advance to the succeeding corners, thus scoring runs as they cross home plate.)
   E. If the batter does not copy the pitcher's pattern exactly or stops in the middle of performing the sequence and begins again, his team is penalized with an "out"; that player then takes his seat and the next team member takes his turn "at bat." (Players already on base do not advance to the next corner if a teammate is declared out.)
   F. Each team is allowed three outs per time at bat (there are no "strikes" in this game), and the winning team is determined after seven innings of play.

4. In order to ensure that one team may not take unfair advantage of the other by memorizing preceding rhythmic sequences, avoid pitching the same pattern to consecutive players.

5. In addition, the playing of the game may be facilitated by choosing a scorekeeper to keep an ongoing record of each team's runs and outs.

6. Depending on the ability of the particular class, you may wish to include more complex rhythmic movement patterns for the players to reproduce correctly, incorporating foot-stomping, finger-snapping, knee-bending, head-nodding, etc.

7. Competent students from each team may eventually be selected as pitchers for the game when they have demonstrated their proficiency at performing the rhythmic sequences.

THUMBPRINT CRITTER PHOTO FOLLIES
Project

Objective: To develop the ability to associate the sound of a particular musical composition with an appropriate mental image.

Grades: 2–4

1. Obtain a recording of *Carnival of the Animals* by Saint-Saëns. (Nine selections from the composition will be used in this particular activity.)

2. Give each student a large sheet of drawing paper, crayons and/or colored pencils, glue or paste, and nine 4" x 6" unlined index cards.

3. Place an open ink pad on your desk and invite the students (two or three at a time) to moisten their thumbs with the ink and press one thumbprint in the center of each of the index cards.

4. Tell the class that, as the various selections of *Carnival of the Animals* are played, each student is to design animals from the thumbprints that are appropriate to the character of the music; each thumbprint will be the "body" of each individual animal, and the students are to use their crayons and/or colored pencils to add the necessary features to complete the animal, such as a head, tail, legs, wings, fins, feathers, etc.

5. When each "critter" has been drawn, the students are to design

background scenes for each of their thumbprint animals, thereby creating make-believe "photographs" ostensibly taken on their summertime outings to the zoo.

6. Each student then mounts his nine thumbprint critter "photos" on the sheet of drawing paper for display in the classroom. (If desired, captions and/or humorous animal names may be printed beneath each index card.)

7. To assist you, the following musical descriptions and suggested animal drawings to accompany the individual selections of *Carnival of the Animals* are included:

A. "Royal March of the Lion" – In this majestic tribute to the "King of Beasts," the roar of the lion is unmistakably expressed by the louder, then softer ascending and descending patterns played on the piano. A tiger, leopard, or panther, however, would also be an appropriate animal for the students to draw as an interpretation of the music of this selection.

B. "Hens and Roosters" – Imitating the cackling of the hens, the piano and the stringed instruments comically describe the antics of these busy fowl as the call of the rooster is announced by the clarinet.

C. "Fleet-Footed Animals" – Horses, ponies, zebra, antelope, and other hoofed inhabitants of the zoo are suggested by the swiftly moving passages played furiously on the piano.

D. "Turtles" – The slow-paced melody of the low tones played by the orchestra depicts the lazy, unhurried gait of the giant tortoises that roam the zoological gardens.

E. "Elephants" – A popular resident of the park, the heavy, lumbering elephant is represented by the deep sounds of the string bass. However, the students' awareness of the weighty character of the music may instead be reflected in drawings of the rhinoceros, hippopotamus, or other cumbersome members of the zoo population.

F. "Kangaroos" – Although the leaping sounds of the piano suggest the locomotion of the kangaroo, additional animals which may be illustrative of this "hopping" music include the rabbit and the frog.

G. "Aquarium" – In a kaleidoscope of motion and color, the exotic tropical fishes are described by the delicate tones of the celesta in combination with soft sounds produced by the piano and the stringed instruments.

H. "The Bird" – Quick, fluttering musical passages played on the flute, piano, and strings are suggestive of the light, rapid movements of the multicolored occupants of the huge zoological aviary.

I. "The Swan" – The elegant swan is portrayed by a smooth melody performed by the cello over a rippling piano accompaniment that represents gently flowing water. Other graceful aquatic creatures which may be envisioned by the students include the seal, otter, dolphin, and whale.

ON THE JOB
Project

Objective: To develop the ability to recognize various musical symbols.

Grades: 3 – 6

1. Give each student a large sheet of drawing paper and crayons and/or colored pencils.

2. Following a class discussion of the meaning and significance of Labor Day, ask the students to name as many different occupations, careers, and professions as they can, and list those vocations on the chalkboard—farmer, teacher, doctor, nurse, truck driver, editor, etc.

3. Explain that a particular picture-symbol may be associated with each of the occupations; call on the students to name appropriate job symbols and list them on the board beside each vocation. For example:

> Policeman – badge
> Librarian – book
> Painter   – brush
> Janitor   – broom

4. Tell the students that the written language of music is also associated with specific visual characters. Draw the following musical symbols and their names on the chalkboard:

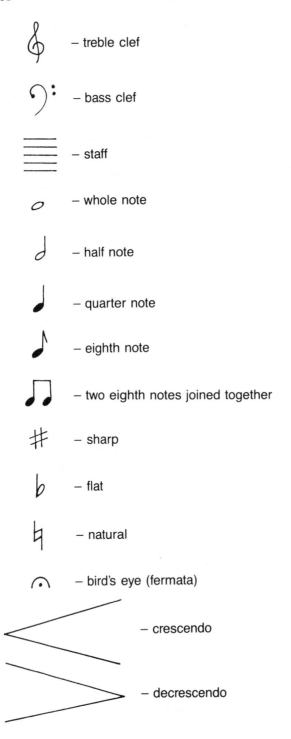

– treble clef

– bass clef

– staff

– whole note

– half note

– quarter note

– eighth note

– two eighth notes joined together

– sharp

– flat

– natural

– bird's eye (fermata)

– crescendo

– decrescendo

5. Direct the class to proceed as follows:
   A. Each student is to select a particular job symbol which he will illustrate on his drawing paper.
   B. In addition, he is to choose one or more of the above musical symbols that he must cleverly conceal within his drawing of the job symbol. (The musical symbols may be drawn in various positions—sideways, upside down, "inside out," etc.—and sizes.)
6. When the illustrations have been completed, the students take turns attempting to discover the various musical symbols hidden within their classmates' job symbols.

MUSICAL POSTCARDS

Project

Objective: To develop the ability to associate the sound of a particular musical composition with an appropriate mental image.

Grades: 3–6

1. Give each student four 4" x 6" unlined index cards and crayons and/or colored pencils.
2. Discuss with the class the various family outings which the students have taken during their summer vacations; tell the students that they will be designing "musical postcards" illustrating the different vacation retreats that they have visited or would like to visit on a future summer holiday.
3. Tell the students that, as they listen to the various recordings that you will play, they are to draw a particular vacation scene on each of their index cards—postcards—appropriate to the character of the music. (You need play only *one* musical composition for each scene to be illustrated, but that recording may be played several times in order to provide the students ample time to finish their drawings.)
4. When the postcards have been completed, the students may wish to "send" them to one another; students' names may be written on the reverse side of the cards which are hidden around the classroom to be found by the addressees.

5. Suggested musical compositions and appropriate postcard scenes include the following:

Musical Compositions	Appropriate Postcard Scenes
"Viennese Musical Clock" from *Háry János Suite*–Kodály	Carnival, fair, amusement park, or circus
Entry of the Gladiators–Fucik	
"Circus Music" from *The Red Pony*–Copland	
Circus Polka–Stravinsky	
Selections from *Under the Big Top*–Donaldson	
"The Pines of the Janiculum" from *The Pines of Rome*–Respighi	Woodland, forest, or mountainous area (for camping, picnicking, exploring, hiking, or horseback riding)
"Cattle" from *The Plow That Broke the Plains*–Thomson	
"On the Trail" from *Grand Canyon Suite*–Grofé	
In the Steppes of Central Asia–Borodin	
"The Moldau" from *My Fatherland*, Opening section –Smetana	Coastline, beach, or lakeside resort (for various water activities)
"The Fountain of Valle Giulia at Dawn" from *The Fountains of Rome*–Respighi	
"Sailing" from *Harbor Vignettes*–Donaldson	
On the Beautiful Blue Danube –J. Strauss	
Selections from *Carnival of the Animals*–Saint-Saëns	Zoo

"GETTING TO KNOW YOU" RHYTHM CIRCLE
Rhythmic Activity

Objective: To develop independent rhythmic response to a particular
beat using a variety of body movements.

Grades: K–3

1. Direct the students to form a large circle; each student should
   stand so he is not touching his neighbor.

2. Stand in the center of the circle and begin a series of body
   movements in a steady rhythm. Tell the students to imitate these.
   For example, you clap your hands together four times and then
   slap your lap four times. Repeat these motions over and over until
   you and the students are clapping and slapping simultaneously
   to the same beat.

3. When the students appear to be following the motions accurately,
   play a recording of bouncy, rhythmic music to provide the beat to
   which you all move.

4. You may change your motions at any time, and the students are to
   take the cue and keep following you. For example, you may drop
   the hand-clapping and lap-slapping and begin stamping your feet
   and snapping your fingers for the next four beats.

5. At any given moment, however, you may abruptly stop the
   rhythmic movements, point to a particular student in the circle,
   and announce, "Left!" or "Right!"

6. The student to whom you point must respond as follows:

   A. If "Left!" is shouted out to him, that student must call out the
      name of the student standing to his left side; if "Right!" is
      called, he must name the neighbor to his right.

   B. In addition, the student must name the designated neighbor
      before you count aloud "one-two-three" in a steady rhythm.

   C. If the student responds correctly, the activity continues as you
      and the class resume your rhythmic motions.

   D. If the student answers incorrectly or fails to respond within the
      allotted time, he is to sit on the floor in the center of the circle
      until he is replaced by another erring student.

7. The activity continues with various students taking turns as
   "leaders" of the rhythmic motions in the center of the circle.

8. Types of recordings suggested for this activity include the following:

Various selections of rhythmic, current popular music

Instrumental recordings for creative movement, motor skills development, and physical fitness

Selections of music for gymnastics, floor exercises, rope jumping and parachute play

SPORTS SHOW

Pantomime

Objective: To develop the ability to use body movements to describe familiar sports.

Grades: K–6

1. Tell the students that each of them is to select a partner; direct the student pairs to scatter around the classroom.
2. Explain to the class that they will be pantomiming *in slow motion* various familiar summertime sports activities that involve at least two people—e.g., baseball, volleyball, tennis, soccer, etc.
3. As you play a recording of appropriate music, one student of each pair is to *initiate* the actions of their selected sport and his partner is to *respond* accordingly. For example, if baseball is the chosen sport, the student who begins the activity may pantomime pitching the ball to his partner who may react by batting the ball back to the pitcher; the pitcher then catches the ball and throws it again to the batter as their slow-motion pantomime continues. (Encourage the students to express their various sports with graceful, exaggerated body movements in order to accurately represent the slow-motion aspect of their pantomimes.)
4. The activity continues in the above manner until you ring a bell, tap a drum, or produce some other distinctive sound; this is the signal for the other partner in each student pair to take a turn at initiating the action.
5. Various students may be called upon to demonstrate their pantomime for the class who are to determine which sport is being described by carefully watching the gestures of the partners.

6. Suitable musical compositions for this activity include the following:

Fanfare for the Common Man–Copland

"Dance of the Hours" from *La Gioconda*–Ponchielli

Nadia's Theme (The Young and the Restless)–De Vorzon and Botkin (recorded on A & M records)

Various additional compositions of instrumental music for interpretative movement, pantomime, and ballet

"WHEN I GROW UP"

Pantomime

Objective: To develop the ability to use body movements to describe familiar jobs, careers, and professions.

Grades: K–3

1. Tell the students to consider "what they want to be when they grow up"; then direct them to scatter around the classroom.

2. As you play a recording of appropriate music, the students are to pantomime the characteristic mannerisms of persons engaged in the particular occupations they are considering for their future careers. For example, the student wishing someday to be a secretary may demonstrate the motions of using a typewriter; a future carpenter might imitate the act of driving a nail into a board.

3. Various students may be called upon to demonstrate their pantomimes for the class who are to determine what their fellow pupils want to be when they grow up by carefully watching the gestures of their classmates.

4. Suitable musical compositions for this activity include the following:

"Pastoral Symphony" from *Messiah*–Handel

"Voiles" from Preludes, Book I–Debussy

"Arabian Dance" from *The Nutcracker Suite*, Op. 71–Tchaikovsky

Various additional compositions of instrumental music for interpretative movement, pantomime, and ballet

2

COLUMBUS DAY

October 12

In fourteen hundred and ninety-two
Columbus sailed the ocean blue.
But a fact that would surely have made old Chris swoon
Is that someday a man would set foot on the moon.

Every year it's the same old story. You open your lesson plan book, turn to the month of October, and scrawl "COLUMBUS DAY–NO SCHOOL" across the appropriate row of squares. Then, you figure that sometime before the holiday you'll have to conduct that dreary class discussion about the discovery of the New World or show your students one of those dull filmstrips on the life and times of Christopher Columbus or *something*. And you think, "What a crummy holiday Columbus Day is" for inspiring any sort of interesting classroom activities.

But read again, if you will, that little rhyme printed above and consider the meaning of Columbus Day in the broadest sense— exploration and discovery; adventure and achievement. What may have been thought to be impossible in Columbus' time might well be considered commonplace today; but, in any age, that characteristically human drive to search and find, to "go where no man has gone before" carries the promise of challenge and excitement. The observance of Columbus Day presents an excellent opportunity for you and your students to acknowledge that bold spirit of adventure—past, present, and future; and an exploratory journey into the world of music will enhance and enliven your commemoration of that October holiday.

For instance, various musical words and their meanings are explored in "Musical Map," a creative new look at that old sea voyage of the fifteenth century. Discovering musical note values—through the eyes of a modern explorer—is emphasized in the intriguing "'Black Whole.'" "Musical Telescopes," an imaginative listening project, encourages the students to envision the vast new horizons first witnessed by Christopher Columbus and those interstellar sights observed by an astronaut piloting the starship Columbus. The concept of north, south, east, and west is investigated in the rhythmic "Compass Shuffle," and "Rock-the-Boat" is a rambunctious venture into the realm of musical instruments. For the genuine outer space buffs in the class, "Space Race" is a captivating intergalactic excursion into the dimensions of musical time and speed.

So, after you've drawn that red circle around October 12 on the classroom calender, leaf through the pages of this chapter and sample a project or prepare a game. Developed from that irresistible blend of music and the holiday theme, the innovative activities that follow are guaranteed to stimulate enthusiastic student participation and transform your class's recognition of Columbus Day from a passive observance into a truly special occasion.

MUSICAL MAP
Bulletin Board Idea

Objective: To develop the ability to recognize various musical words and their meanings.

Grades: 4–6

1. Prepare for this activity by covering the bulletin board with plain background paper.
2. List the following musical words and their meanings on the chalkboard:

Allegro	– fast, quick
Largo	– slow
Vivace	– brisk, lively
Poco	– little
Brusco	– harsh, rough
Furioso	– wild, furious
Misterioso	– mysterious
Grandioso	– majestic
Calmato	– quiet, tranquil
Subito	– sudden
Fermata	– a pause; hold
Octet	– a composition for or performance by eight persons

3. Give each student a large sheet of drawing paper and crayons or oil-based pastel crayons.

4. With the students, examine the classroom wall map of the world, taking special note of map features such as continents, oceans, islands, etc. Discuss the similarities and differences in detail between modern world maps and those that Christopher Columbus may have used to chart his voyage across the Atlantic Ocean.

5. After having concluded that the geographical concept of the world at that point in history was based largely on ignorance and superstition, the students should name those details which may have appeared on nautical maps of Columbus' time. Write these in a second list on the chalkboard—e.g., large land masses, bodies of water, islands, sailing ships, mermaids, sea monsters, treacherous ocean currents, areas of storms, "the edge of the world," etc.

6. Direct the class to design a "musical map" of Columbus' voyage as follows:

   A. Each student is to select an item from the list of map details— e.g., sailing ship—and write its name in a corner of the drawing paper.

   B. He then considers the various characteristics of his selected map detail, chooses a word from the list of musical terms which could be used as an appropriate name for that item, and writes that term on his paper. For example, since a good sailing vessel is one that is fast and sleek, the musical word *allegro* could certainly be descriptive of that particular map detail; hence, the name "Allegro" for the sailing ship.

C. On the remaining portion of his drawing paper, the student is then to illustrate and appropriately label his particular map detail; for example, ALLEGRO is printed prominently on the bow of the ship.

7. To complete the activity, the individual drawings are then cut out with scissors, and, in groups of two or three at a time, invite the students to attach their map details to the bulletin board. (The large land masses, oceans, and the smaller waterways may be drawn and labeled directly on the background paper rather than attached as separate items.)

8. Sample musical map details, their descriptions, and appropriate names for use in this activity include the following:

BRUSCO Straits–Columbus and his men must summon all their courage to enter these *rough* waters.

MISTERIOSO Rectangle–Not unlike the infamous "Bermuda Triangle," this dreaded area of the ocean is fraught with all sorts of *puzzling* dangers.

FERMATA Island–Columbus' sailors may *pause* at this haven of rest before continuing on their perilous voyage.

CALMATO Lagoon–A secluded and inviting cove, this small inlet of water is *quiet* and *peaceful*.

OCTET Sea Monster–This terrifying *eight*-legged creature is a legendary threat to those who dare to invade its watery domain.

FURIOSO Tempest–Howling winds, heavy seas, and torrential rains await the unlucky sailors who venture into this *wild* storm.

THE "BLACK WHOLE"
Bulletin Board Idea

Objective: To develop the ability to recognize various musical notes.

Grades: 1–6

1. Prepare for this activity by covering the bulletin board with plain background paper.

2. List the following musical notes, their names, and arbitrary numerical values on the chalkboard:

O – whole note – 4

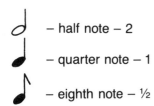

♩ – half note – 2

♩ – quarter note – 1

♪ – eighth note – ½

3. Select a capable student to draw a *large* whole note in the center of the background paper with crayons or paints. Have him sketch three concentric rings around the whole note, and, in accordance with the theme of the "black whole," have him completely fill in the whole note using black colored crayons or paints. (At this point, you should emphasize that, although there is no such musical symbol as a "black"—filled in—whole note, an imaginary "black whole" is being designed for use in this activity.)

4. Explain that each musical note is always assigned a specific numerical value for the purposes of rhythm; then tell the class that they will be drawing various "note" interplanetary objects in each of the circles concentric with the black whole. In the ring nearest the black whole, the students are to illustrate starships, meteorites, rockets, satellites, etc. on which they are to draw *half* notes; in the adjoining ring, space objects labeled with *quarter* notes; in the ring farthest from the center, objects marked with *eighth* notes.

5. Working at the bulletin board in groups of two or three at a time, the students continue drawing until the three rings are filled with all types of interplanetary craft and objects, each labeled with the appropriate musical note. (To maintain the mathematical relationship of the notes, different numbers of space objects are to be drawn within the rings; i.e., since the quarter note is of lesser numerical value than the half note, the middle ring should contain a greater number of space objects than the circle nearest the black whole; in the outside ring, the amount of eighth note objects is to exceed that of the quarter note circle.)

6. For older or more advanced students, you may wish to use the following table of musical notes as the basis for this activity:

𝅝 – whole note – 4

𝅗𝅥• – dotted half note – 3

𝅗𝅥 – half note – 2

♩. — dotted quarter note — 1½

♩ — quarter note — 1

♪ — eighth note — ½

♪ — sixteenth note — ¼

SPACE RACE

Game

Objective: To develop an awareness of common musical words and symbols that pertain to time, repetition, and speed (tempo).

Grades: 3 – 6 (two – four players)

1. You (or a selected student) enlarge the game playing field on page 41 on a large sheet of oaktag, posterboard, or drawing paper.

2. Gather together the following items to be used in playing the game:

   A. One die

   B. Two to four different-colored game markers to be used for movement around the board

3. Instruct the students how to play the game as follows:

   A. The object of the game is to be the first player to complete a "flight" through one of the note tracks, successfully arriving at the appropriate space "base."

   B. Having positioned their markers on their chosen note starting circles, the players are ready to roll the die and begin the game. When each player "lands on" a space of the track designated by markings other than or in addition to the note symbols, he is to proceed accordingly:

Space on the Track	Procedure
A time signature – $\dfrac{2}{4}$, $\dfrac{3}{4}$, $\dfrac{4}{4}$, $\dfrac{6}{8}$	Go back to the starting circle and begin the game over.

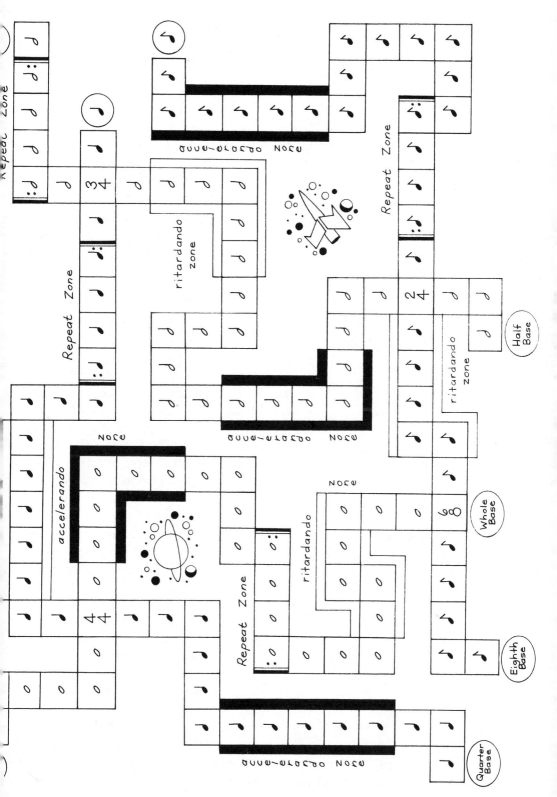

41

The four spaces enclosed within the ‖: :‖ symbols and designated as the "Repeat Zone"

Move back to the first space entered in the zone and remain there until a number is rolled on the die large enough to completely clear *all four spaces*. For example, if a player lands in the third space of the Repeat Zone, he must automatically back up to the first space of the zone and remain there until he rolls a "four," "five," or "six" to pass through the area and continue along the track.

The five spaces designated as the "Accelerando Zone"

On the next turn, *double* the number rolled on the die and proceed along the track. When a player lands anywhere within this zone, he "speeds up" by doubling the number of his *next* roll and continuing along the track. (If necessary, this procedure is repeated on each successive roll until the player clears the zone.)

The five spaces designated as the "Ritardando Zone"

On the next turn, *reduce* the number rolled on the die by *one* and proceed along the track. When a player lands anywhere within this zone, he "slows down" by reducing the number of his *next* roll by one and continuing along the track. (If necessary, this procedure is repeated on each successive roll until the player clears the zone.)

4. In order to facilitate movement around the board, the three zones may be designed in various colors—e.g., the spaces of the Repeat

Zone may be colored blue; the spaces of the Accelerando Zone, green; the spaces of the Ritardando Zone, red.

5. To provide an attractive "galactic" appearance to the playing field, additional spaceships, planets, stars, meteorites, etc. may be illustrated on the game board.

ROCK-THE-BOAT

Game

Objective: To develop familiarity with the names of various musical instruments.

Grades: 2 – 4 (entire class participation)

1. List the names of familiar musical instruments on the chalkboard:

Piano	Clarinet
Violin	Rhythm sticks
Drum	Tambourine
Flute	Guitar
Trumpet	Trombone
Organ	Tuba
Bells	Harp

2. Prepare *two* sets of unlined index cards; label the cards in each set with names taken from the above list of musical instruments. Each set (which consists of enough cards for *half* the members of the class) should contain the names of the *same* instruments so that the two sets are identical.

3. Distribute the prepared cards to all but one of the students; tell them to keep the identities of their instruments secret and to sit in a large circle on the floor.

4. Assign the remaining student the task of serving as "Captain Columbus" and direct him to stand in the center of the circle.

5. Explain to the class how to play the game as follows:

   A. The Captain calls out the name of one of the musical instruments listed on the board.

   B. The two students in the circle holding the cards labeled with the announced instrument must then jump up, quickly exchange places with each other, and sit down on the floor again.

C. Meanwhile, the Captain is to rush from the center of the circle in an attempt to fill the place vacated by one of the students in possession of that particular instrument card.

D. Of the three moving students, the one who is left without a place to sit in the circle becomes the Captain for the next round of play. (If a student is holding an instrument card at the time he becomes the Captain, he must relinquish that card to one of the students who found a place to sit in the circle. A student never keeps possession of a card when he performs the role of Captain.)

6. To avoid problems, you should make certain at the outset that an even number of students will be sitting in the circle so that the pairing of instrument names will be possible. Any "extra" student who would offset the balance may be rotated into and out of the game at various intervals, substituting for fellow players.

7. Musical instrument names are not the only terms that may be used in this particular classroom activity. Names of composers, musical symbols, song titles, musical words, singers, rock groups, etc., are also suitable for similar games.

MUSICAL TELESCOPES

Project

Objective: To develop the ability to associate the sound of a particular musical composition with an appropriate mental image.

Grades: 2 – 4

In preparation for this activity, have the students bring cardboard paper towel tubes from home. You must also prepare by reading Step 5, selecting *one musical example for each telescope scene*, and recording excerpts from those compositions on tape. This particular tape will then be used as the accompaniment for the students' smooth, uninterrupted viewing through their "musical telescopes."

1. In addition to the cardboard tube, give each student a pencil, ruler, scissors, cellophane tape, two 3" x 5" unlined index cards, and crayons and/or colored pencils.

2. Discuss with the class the various sights that Christopher Columbus may have viewed through his spyglass as he voyaged across the Atlantic Ocean; also consider the scenes that a modern day

Columbus—i.e, astronaut—might observe through the telescope on his spaceship as he explores the heavens.

3. Tell the class that they will be fashioning their own "telescopes" to focus on the "scenes" viewed both by Christopher Columbus and a modern space explorer as follows:

A. Making the *telescope*

1. Using a pencil and ruler, each student is to measure one inch from an end of his cardboard tube and mark off that distance all around the tube with dots.

2. He then connects the dots with a line, punctures the tube with the scissors, and cuts along the line, leaving a one-half inch portion of the line uncut. (The uncut section of the tube is to be reinforced with several pieces of tape placed both inside and outside the tube.)

B. Making the *scene strips* (This procedure is to be followed for *both* index cards, resulting in *two* separate scene strips.)

1. Each student is to fold and then cut his index card in half lengthwise and overlap the two sections by one-half inch at the short ends; he seams the ends securely with several pieces of tape, forming a strip approximately nine inches in length.

2. Marking off one-half inch on each end of the strip for margins, the student then sets the telescope tube perpendicular to the index card strip. Using the open end of the tube as a pattern, he traces four circles, side by side, onto the strip, leaving a space between each circle and avoiding drawing the circles on the taped middle seam.

3. The student is then to illustrate a specific telescope scene in each of the eight circles that is descriptive of the sound of the various musical compositions which you play as follows:

a. As one of the compositions is played, the student begins designing an appropriate scene observed by Columbus in the far left circle of one of his card strips.

b. As the *same* compositon is played a second time, he is to illustrate a scene viewed from the telescope of an astronaut's spaceship in the far left circle of the other card strip.

c. As the next musical composition is played, the circle immediately to the right of the first is illustrated on each strip, and the drawing continues as described above until all eight circles are filled with appropriate scenes. (The order in which you recorded the excerpts on the tape is the *same* order in which the sample musical compositions are to be played for the students to illustrate.)

4. Direct the students to use their musical telescopes as follows:

   A. Holding the uncut, reinforced section of the tube downward, each student places the opposite end of the telescope in front of his eye.

   B. He inserts the left end of one of the scene strips into the tube slot and pulls it toward the left until the first circle scene appears in the end of the tube when the telescope is held up to a bright light.

   C. As you play the tape recording of the excerpts of the selected musical compositions, the appropriate scenes are pulled into view from right to left. (The second scene strip is inserted and drawn through the tube in the same manner as the tape is played again.)

5. Suggested musical compositions and appropriate telescope scenes include the following:

Musical Compositions	Appropriate Telescope Scenes – Columbus	Appropriate Telescope Scenes – Astronaut
"Neptune" from *The Planets*, Op. 32 – Holst "The Swan of Tuonela" from *Four Legends from "The Kalevala,"* Op. 22 – Sibelius	Dolphins gliding lazily over gentle waves as the sun rises over a tranquil sea	Glittering stars and shining planets set against the silent expanse of endless, black space
"Mars" from *The Planets*, Op. 32 – Holst "Dialogue of the Wind and the Sea" from *La Mer* (The Sea) – Debussy	Rolling black clouds, churning waves, and the drenching rain of a sudden ocean storm	The huge, wildly spinning rocks of a deadly asteroid field

Musical Compositions	Appropriate Telescope Scenes – Columbus	Appropriate Telescope Scenes – Astronaut
The Banshee – Cowell Any suitable electronic music recording – e.g., *Poème électronique* – Varèse	An abandoned, battered "ghost" sailing ship	An ominous, alien unidentified flying object
"War March of the Priests" from *Athalie* – Mendelssohn "Main Title" (Theme) from *Superman* – Williams (recorded on Warner Brothers Records)	A shoreline with lush vegetation and an inviting port signifying the successful completion of a perilous voyage	The shimmering planet Earth, which indicates home to the weary space traveler

THE COMPASS SHUFFLE

Rhythmic Activity

Objective: To develop independent rhythmic response to a particular beat using a variety of body movements.

Grades: K – 3

1. Direct the students to scatter around the classroom; each student is to stand so he is not touching his neighbor, and all the students are to face in the *same* direction.

2. Tell the class that, as you play a recording of bouncy, rhythmic music, they are to begin inventing various original rhythmic gestures to the beat of the music; for example, finger-snapping, hand-clapping, thigh-slapping, or combinations of movements.

3. Explain further that when you ring a bell and call out a particular compass direction, the students are to respond appropriately as follows:

   If "north" is announced, each student is to *walk forward*.

   If "south" is announced, each student is to *walk backward*.

   If "east" is announced, each student is to *move sideways to the right*.

If "west" is announced, each student is to *move sideways to the left.*

4. The students are to continue their rhythmic movements as they respond to each announced direction, and are to *keep moving in that direction* until another direction is called out. (To avoid collisions among the students, tell the class that *small* rhythmic steps are to be taken in each announced compass direction.)

5. Variations of this activity include the following:

   A. The students are to scatter around the classroom; each student faces the direction of *his choice* at the beginning of the activity.

   B. Each student selects a partner with whom he can perform "The Compass Shuffle." (If the partners stand side by side while performing, they will be moving in the *same* directions according to your call; if they face one another, they will move in *opposite* directions.)

6. Types of recordings suggested for this activity include the following:

   Various selections of rhythmic, current popular music

   Instrumental recordings for creative movement, motor skills development, and physical fitness

   Selections of music for gymnastics, floor exercises, rope jumping, and parachute play

3

HALLOWEEN

October 31

Without doubt, Halloween is the holiday of holidays in the elementary classroom. Of course, there is the special, glowing excitement of Christmas, and the festivity of Valentine's Day dispels the doldrums of the long winter months; but no single holiday event from September through June captures the students' imaginations more than dressing up in fanciful costumes and marching from classroom to classroom in the annual Halloween parade. Whether they are attired in store-bought outfits of shiny fabric and paper masks or decked out in those elaborate homemade fashions that Mom spent hours designing, elementary students of all ages fairly tingle with anticipation of the traditional thrills and chills of Halloween. Add the refreshing musical activities of this chapter to the students' already buoyant mood, and you and your class will experience a most memorable October 31.

The spooky sounds of Halloween, for example, are represented by musical symbols in "The Haunted House," a tantalizing game in which the "terrified" players must pass through the rooms of an eerie mansion where "things go bump in the night." To acquaint the students with classic musical compositions that describe particular Halloween legends and devilish celebrations, "Musical Tombstones" and "Haunted Mountains" are most enjoyable projects. "Herb, the

Ghost," a jolly little fellow, teaches the younger students to recognize and identify common musical symbols, and in constructing "Haunted Musical Instrument Castles," the class members combine their artistic efforts as they engage in a very unusual encounter with the four families of musical instruments. For a lot of rhythmic action at the class Halloween party, "The Goblin's Touch," "Monster Limbo," and "Witch's Broom Boogie" are three fun-filled activities that contribute to the "spirit" of the occasion.

To the elementary student, the preparation for Halloween is nearly as exciting as the arrival of the day itself. Capitalize on that natural enthusiasm by making music an integral part of your holiday plans. Enjoy a musical activity with your youngsters after the orange paper jack-o'-lanterns have been taped to the classroom windows. Play a musical game or two when all of the black pipe cleaner spiders are securely dangling from the ceiling; and have a happy Halloween!

HAUNTED MUSICAL INSTRUMENT CASTLES
Bulletin Board Idea

Objective: To develop an awareness of the four families of musical instruments.

Grades: 4 – 6

1. Prepare for this activity by covering the bulletin board with plain background paper.
2. Draw four *large*, three-dimensional squares on the background and label each with one of the following names:

   > Brass Castle
   > Percussion Palace
   > String Fortress
   > Woodwind Mansion

3. After presenting a brief unit study of the four families of musical instruments, list the families on the chalkboard:

   > Brass
   > Percussion
   > String
   > Woodwind

4. Ask the students to name as many members of the four families as they can, and list those examples on the chalkboard:

Brass	**String**
Trumpet	Violin
Cornet	Cello
Trombone	String bass
Tuba	Viola
French horn	Harp
Baritone horn	Banjo
Sousaphone	Guitar
Bugle	
Percussion	**Woodwind**
Piano	Flute
Gong	Clarinet
Kettledrum	Oboe
Cymbals	Bassoon
Castanets	Piccolo
Tambourine	Saxophone
Snare drum	English horn
Triangle	Organ
Bass drum	
Xylophone	
Chimes	

5. Give each student scissors, glue or paste, crayons and/or colored pencils, and a large sheet of drawing paper.

6. Tell the students that each of them is to select several instruments or parts of instruments from the above lists and illustrate those instruments and/or parts on the drawing paper. (The students may find it necessary to scan their music texts or search through the school library for pictures or photographs of musical instruments on which to model their drawings; tell the students that they need not extensively detail their illustrations—just the general shape of the instruments and a few characteristic features are necessary. In addition, the size of each drawing is to be appropriate to the dimensions of the castles.)

7. When the drawings are completed, the students are to cut them out with scissors.

8. Working in groups of two or three at a time, the students then arrange and attach their instruments and instrument parts onto the appropriate squares of the bulletin board forming "castles." Direct the students to position and paste their musical instruments and parts onto the squares in such a way as to create

walls, towers, doors, roofs, chimneys, turrets, dormers, cupolas, shutters, parapets, balconies, archways, drawbridges, etc. For example, ranks[1] of organ pipes may be situated as parapets edging the balconies of Woodwind Mansion; the main entrance to String Fortress might be formed by the body[2] of a guitar or violin; Percussion Palace may be entered via a piano keyboard drawbridge spanning the moat; clusters of trumpet bells[3] of varying heights may be set vertically on end to simulate the towers and turrets of Brass Castle.

9. The activity continues until each castle is an attractive composite of the various members of the appropriate instrument families. Thus, each student may contribute several musical instruments and instrument parts to the formation of all four castles. (You may find it necessary to guide the students in the most desirable placement of their drawings.)

10. When all of the castles have been formed, you or a selected student(s) fills in with crayons or colored pencils any gaps remaining in the composites; then invite all of the students to add the following finishing touches to the scene:

A. Assorted Halloween characters are drawn, cut out, and attached in and around the castles—e.g., wide-eyed owls, vampire bats, and grinning ghosts may soar from rooftops and balconies; bristly black cats might perch on tower windowsills; wart-nosed witches, toothy goblins, and other freaky folk may frolic among the tombstones in the palace cemetery; plump toads and hairy spiders might lurk in the shadows beneath the drawbridge, etc.

B. If desired, various musical symbols may be added in different sizes and positions to lend a final musical touch to the scene—

e.g., eighth notes with enlarged flags ♪ might be set atop the

turrets as pennants; staffs ≣ turned vertically on end may be

drawn in tower windows as bars; various notes 𝅝, 𝅗𝅥, 𝅘𝅥 might be grouped together to form the trees and shrubbery of the palace grounds, etc.

---

[1]Rank – a set of organ pipes.

[2]Body – the sound box of a stringed instrument.

[3]Bell – the bell-shaped opening of a wind or brass instrument.

11. To accommodate younger students, *one* castle may be designed on the bulletin board, combining all four families of musical instruments and adding the spooky Halloween effects.

THE HAUNTED HOUSE

Game

Objective: To develop an awareness of common musical symbols that pertain to loudness and softness (dynamics).

Grades: 2 – 5 (two – four players)

1. List the following musical symbols and their meanings on the chalkboard:

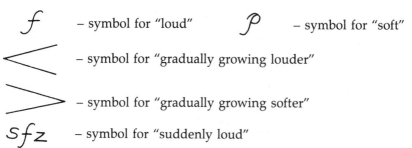

f – symbol for "loud" p – symbol for "soft"

$<$ – symbol for "gradually growing louder"

$>$ – symbol for "gradually growing softer"

sfz – symbol for "suddenly loud"

2. You (or a selected student) enlarge the game playing field on page 53 on a large sheet of oaktag, posterboard, or drawing paper.

3. Gather together the following items to be used in playing the game:

   A. Two to four different-colored game markers to be used for movement around the board.

   B. One game spinner, prepared as follows:

   1. Invert a paper plate, and, using a marking pen, divide it into eight sections; puncture a hole in the center of the plate, and label the sections with the musical symbols shown on page 53.

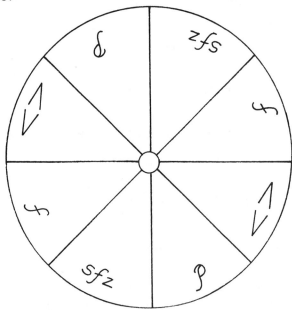

   2. From cardboard or oaktag, cut an arrow shape of appropriate size and puncture a hole in the center of the arrow.

   3. Line up the two holes; place the arrow onto the labeled side of the plate; attach the arrow *very loosely* to the plate with a paper fastener (brad) so that it may be spun freely around the disc.

4. On the chalkboard, list the eight Halloween sound words printed in the "windows" of the haunted house game board. Discuss with the class how each sound word may be associated with one or more of the musical symbols previously listed on the chalkboard. For example, since a moan is a sound that begins quietly, rises to a

louder volume, and then dies away, the symbols $<$

and $>$ would be appropriately descriptive of that particular sound word. The musical symbols (omitting sfz) are then matched to and drawn beside each Halloween sound word on the chalkboard:

bump –	p
howl –	f
thud –	p
scream –	f
creak –	p
wail –	$<>$
shriek –	f
moan –	$<>$

5. Tell the students how to play the game as follows:

   A. The object of the game is to pass through all the numbered "rooms" of the haunted house, beginning and ending at the "front door."

   B. Having positioned their markers on the front door of the house, the players are ready to activate the spinner and begin the game.

   C. In order to advance to each successive room, the player must spin the musical symbol(s) that matches the sound word printed in the window of that particular room. For instance, to move into the "bump" room, the player must spin a p symbol on the paper plate.

   D. If he fails to spin the symbol required for entrance into the next room, the player must remain in his present location until he does spin the appropriate symbol.

   E. If, at any time, the player spins the symbol sfz , he is "suddenly frightened by a loud noise" which sends him bolting back to the front door from where he must begin the game over; in addition, the player must spin the sfz symbol in order to pass from Room #8 to the front door, thereby successfully completing the game.

6. To create a delightfully devilish atmosphere in which to play the game, the spinner and playing field (decorated with a host of colorful Halloween personalities and effects) may be designed in part with special fluorescent crayons; the game may then be played in a darkened area of the classroom, illuminated only by an ultraviolet light.

HERB, THE GHOST

Game

Objective: To develop the ability to recognize various musical symbols.

Grades: 1 – 3 (entire class participation)

1. Draw the following musical symbols and their names on the chalkboard; pronounce each name and allow the symbols and terms to remain on the board for a few days until the students become familiar with them:

    – eighth note

    – bass clef

    – half note

    – staff

    – quarter note

    – treble clef

    – whole note

    – bird's eye (fermata)

2. Then construct the equipment needed for the activity:

   A. Making the *ghost*

      1. Using the following drawing as a model, enlarge the ghost to a height of eighteen inches on a sheet of stiff construction paper or oaktag; the white rectangle in the mouth area is to be increased in size to 2″ x 3½″:

      2. Cut two 3½″ slits in the rectangular section—one slit at the top edge of the rectangle, the other at the bottom edge.

   B. Making the *symbol strips* (Several strips may be required for the activity.)

      1. Cut a strip of construction paper eighteen inches long and three and one-half inches wide.

      2. Rule off the strip into nine 2″ sections and label the "top" and "bottom." Leaving the bottom section blank, draw one musical symbol from the above list in each remaining section of the strip. See the illustration on page 58.

3. Having prepared the ghost and symbol strip(s), you "activate" Herb as follows:

   A. From the underside of the ghost, insert the bottom edge of the symbol strip through the top slit of the white rectangle in Herb's mouth.

   B. Drawing the strip downward on the front side of the ghost, insert it thorough the bottom slit of the rectangle; pull the strip

top

♪

𝄢

♩

≣

♩

𝄞

○

☉

bottom

through to Herb's underside until the first musical symbol appears in the rectangular area of the ghost's mouth.

   C. Continue drawing the strip through Herb's mouth, revealing one musical symbol at a time.

4. When Herb, the Ghost has been prepared and the students have become fairly proficient at identifying the musical symbols on the chalkboard, you are ready to begin the game.

5. Divide the students into two teams; each team sits in a line on the floor. Sit between the teams, hold Herb in your lap, and pull the first musical symbol into view.

6. Call upon the first member of one team to identify that particular symbol. If he names it correctly, one point is awarded to his team; if he answers incorrectly or fails to respond within a reasonable amount of time, the first student of the other team is given the opportunity to correctly name the musical symbol.

7. The game proceeds as described above until every member of both teams has been given the opportunity to correctly identify a symbol; the team that earns the most points is declared to be the winner of the game. (In case of a tie, play may be continued until one team member errs, thereby causing the game to be won by the opposing team.)

Instead of using this activity for team competition, Herb, the Ghost may simply be used by individual students or pairs of students in the same manner as flashcards, providing an enjoyable tool with which the class may learn to recognize and name the various musical symbols.

HAUNTED MOUNTAINS

Project

Objective: To develop familiarity with a classic composition of musical literature.

Grades: 2 – 6

In preparation for this activity, gather enough styrofoam drinking cups for *half* the members of the class. Using scissors, divide each cup in half, cutting down one side of the cup, across the bottom, and up the other side.

1. Give each student one small sheet of drawing paper, one half of a styrofoam cup, scraps of colored construction paper, brown or gray tempera paint, a brush, scissors, glue or paste, and crayons.

2. On the chalkboard, place the name of the musical composition (and the composer) to which the students will be listening:

Night on Bald Mountain – Mussorgsky

3. In your "scariest" voice, tell the story of *Night on Bald Mountain*[4] to the class:

A long time ago, a frightful ceremony took place on a mountain in Russia. Late one night, as the townspeople in the valley below slept peacefully, a terrible sound rumbled across the black sky. An unearthly green light spun down through the darkness and began circling the mountaintop. Suddenly, out of the light loomed a ghastly devil with enormous batlike wings. Stretching forth his arms, the hideous bat-devil called out in a thunderous voice, beckoning the spirits of darkness to gather on the mountain for an evil festival.

A cold, foul-smelling wind arose and began to sweep over Bald Mountain. From the depths of the earth below, all manner of wicked spirits and creatures of the night hastily made their way to the barren slope. Witches on broomsticks sped across the sky. Grinning skeletons riding on horses made only of white bones rattled up the rocky cliffs. Ghosts with glowing eyes rose from the village graveyard as a company of goblins, vampires, and other horrid demons scampered about the rocks and ridges.

The vile creatures began to dance, prancing wildly around a huge fire which blazed on the mountain. Cackling with evil delight, the witches stirred up a cauldron of bubbling brew, and the crazed demons drank greedily. Carrying a mammoth goblet, the witches served the magical potion to the bat-devil who gloated over the unholy celebration from the mountaintop. In one great gulp, the devil swallowed the brew and hurled the goblet into the fire, sending a massive column of flame roaring skyward.

The mountain glowed eerily, teeming with the pagan creatures who leaped and raced about in their horrible madness. Shrieking fiercely and shouting dreadful curses, the demons grew wilder, dashing their mugs of potion against the mountainside. All of a sudden, from the village below, the bell of the tiny town church began to toll in soft, clear tones. Daybreak was at hand.

With a mighty shudder at the approach of dawn, the bat-devil spread his giant wings and flew off into the darkness. In a

---

[4]This version of *Night on Bald Mountain* has been compiled from several interpretations of the story. Specific details may vary from source to source.

rush of fear, the host of evil spirits also took flight, frantically scrambling into their underground dwellings to escape from the light of day. All became very still on Bald Mountain, and the townsfolk nestled in the valley below awoke to the chiming of the bell and a bright, new day.

4. Direct each student to paint the outside of his styrofoam cup half and allow it to dry thoroughly.

5. Next, have each student place a generous amount of glue along the cut edges of the cup half and attach it (bottom up) to the sheet of drawing paper; this results in a three-dimensional "mountain" set against the flat sheet of paper. (A bit of additional time is then required for the glue to dry.)

6. Explain to the class that, as you play a recording of *Night on Bald Mountain*, each student is to create his own original interpretation of the devilish celebration as follows:

   A. On the sheet of drawing paper, the student designs an appropriate background scene for his mountain—e.g., the cemetery, church, and village houses and shops may be sketched in the foreground around the base of the mountain; the thick, dark clouds of the starless nighttime sky might be drawn behind the mountain top; smaller peaks may be illustrated surrounding Bald Mountain, etc.

   B. From the construction paper scraps, each student then fashions the various demons of darkness which he attaches to the surface of the painted cup half; the bat-devil may be constructed in such a way as to stand freely—in three-dimensional style—on the peak.

7. When all of the mountain pictures have been completed, play the recording a second time, providing the opportunity for the students to visualize the bizarre events described in *Night on Bald Mountain* as they listen to the musical composition.

MUSICAL TOMBSTONES
Project

Objective: To develop familiarity with a classic composition of musical literature.

Grades: 4 – 6

1. Give each student two large sheets of drawing paper, scissors, cellophane tape, crayons, and a pencil.

2. On the chalkboard, place the name of the musical composition (and the composer) to which the students will be listening, and list the descriptions of the five scenes[5] which are depicted by the music:

Danse Macabre – Saint Saëns

Scene A – The village clock strikes twelve—midnight! An assortment of ghostly characters begins to gather in the town cemetery for a fiendish celebration.

Scene B – Death (appearing in the form of a skeleton) sits atop a tombstone and tunes his fiddle.

Scene C – The witches, goblins, skeletons, and other spirits of the night break into a wild dance.

Scene D – Gusts of chilly wind begin to moan as the dance of the creatures grows faster and more frantic.

Scene E – The sudden crow of a rooster interrupts the frolicking demons, warning them of the coming dawn; all of the creatures madly scatter to escape from the light of day.

3. Direct the students to proceed as follows:

A. Each student places one sheet of drawing paper directly on top of the other, making certain that all edges are even. He then tapes one of the short ends of the sheets together to form a hinge.

B. The student cuts through both thicknesses of paper with a scissors to round off the corners of the hinged end; this results in a shape similar to that of a tombstone.

C. On the top sheet of paper, each student draws five large squares in a well-spaced arrangement.

D. Being careful to work only on the top sheet, the student then cuts along the two sides and the bottom edge of each square. He folds upward along the attached top edge of the square, forming a flap that may be lifted up to reveal the sheet of paper directly underneath.

E. The student firmly folds all five flaps upward and consecutively numbers the underside of each flap. The outside edges of the tombstone are then securely closed with tape.

4. Explain to the students that, as you play a recording of *Danse*

---

[5]This version of *Danse Macabre* has been compiled from several interpretations of the story. Specific details may vary from source to source.

Macabre, they are to illustrate each of the five scenes described in the musical composition and listed on the chalkboard. One scene is to be designed in each of the squares beneath the numbered flaps.

5. As the students work, they are to listen for the ways in which the scenes are related by the music, and you should point out the manner in which this is accomplished. For example:

Scene A – The "witching hour" is announced by twelve distinct tones played by the harp to suggest the striking of a clock.

Scene B – The abrupt entrance of the flat-sounding violin heralds the arrival of Death who tunes his fiddle.

Scene C – Two waltzlike melodies usher in the strains of the dance. Played initially by the flute, the first melody is somewhat sharp and mechanical; the second, as performed by the violin, is flowing and rather sad. Both melodies banter back and forth, and the exchange is punctuated by the rattling sounds of the xylophone (in imitation of the skeletons' bones).

Scene D – As the melodies intertwine, the rising and falling passages played by the stringed instruments depict the rushing gusts of wind.

Scene E – The call of the rooster is imitated by the oboe, and a pensive final pattern is performed by the violin. All then becomes silent.

6. When all five scenes have been illustrated, the student folds all of the flaps downward, covering the drawings.

7. Play the recording a second time, and have the students lift the appropriate flaps on their tombstones, revealing each successive scene as it is described by the music.

8. Before presenting this activity to the class, however, you should obtain a recording of *Danse Macabre* and listen to it several times. Although it is not necessary for you to determine the exact moment when each musical description ends and another begins, you should become fairly familiar with the composition so you have some idea of how to listen for the various pictures brought to mind by the music. (It is not, however, vital that the students time their drawing with the entrances of the various scenes. As long as they are made aware of when these scenes occur, they may take all the time they need to make attractive illustrations.)

THE GOBLIN'S TOUCH
Rhythmic Activity

Objective: To develop independent rhythmic response to a particular beat using a variety of body movements.

Grades: K – 3

1. Assign every member of the class a particular number which is to be kept secret by each student.
2. Have the students scatter around the classroom.
3. As you play a recording of bouncy, rhythmic music, the students are to begin walking about the room to the beat of the music; each student creates his own rhythmic motions as he walks.
4. When all of the students are walking and moving to the beat, call out one of the assigned numbers. This is the signal for the student with that number to become the "Goblin" who prowls about the room in search of "victims." The Goblin taps various classmates on the shoulder, "paralyzing" those students who must stop all motion and strike a pose.
5. After the Goblin has roamed about the classroom for several moments, turn down the volume of the recording, indicating that the "curse" of the Goblin has been removed.
6. Turn up the volume and the activity continues as the students resume their motions around the room and you announce another number.
7. To vary the activity, the Goblin may touch each victim in a particular area—e.g., the knee. The victim is then required to walk around the classroom and move to the beat of the music with his hand on the touched spot—knee—for the remainder of that round of play.
8. Types of recordings suggested for this activity include the following:

   Various selections of rhythmic, current popular music

   Instrumental recordings for creative movement, motor skills development, and physical fitness

   Selections of music for gymnastics, floor exercises, rope jumping, and parachute play

MONSTER LIMBO
Rhythmic Activity

Objective: To develop independent rhythmic response to a particular beat using a variety of body movements.

Grades: K – 4

1. Select two students to face each other and hold a broom horizontally over their heads at arm's length.

2. Direct the remaining students to form a line facing the horizontal broom.

3. As you play a recording of bouncy, rhythmic music, the students begin creating their own "monster moves" to the beat of the music. While they move rhythmically to the music, the students are to engage in heavy, lumbering, monsterlike gestures.

4. On a given signal from you, the line of rhythmically moving monsters begins walking underneath the broom.

5. As the line of monsters completes each successive pass beneath the broom, the students holding the broom lower it approximately two inches. (Your close supervision is necessary at this point to ensure that the broom is lowered evenly by the same amount each time.)

6. With each pass, the risk of touching the broom with part of the body increases, and any student who does come in direct contact with the broom is declared to be "out" of the Monster Limbo competition. (When the broom has been lowered to within a few inches of the floor, the monsters may find it necessary to modify their movements in order to successfully pass beneath it; in fact, during the last few rounds of the activity, the students may need to abandon their monster gestures and literally crawl through the remaining space.)

7. The student who successfully clears the limbo broom each time (or the last student to touch the broom as he passes below it) is declared to be the "Monster Limbo Champion."

8. Types of recordings suggested for this activity include the following:

   Various selections of rhythmic, current popular music and specific calypso-limbo tunes—e.g., *Limbo Rock*

Instrumental recordings for creative movement, motor skills development, and physical fitness

Selections of music for gymnastics, floor exercises, rope jumping, and parachute play

WITCH'S BROOM BOOGIE
Rhythmic Activity

Objective: To develop independent rhythmic response to a particular beat using a variety of body movements.

Grades: K – 3

1. Choose one student to hold a broom and stand in the center of the classroom.
2. Tell the remaining students that each of them is to select a partner; direct the student pairs to scatter around the room.
3. As you play a recording of bouncy, rhythmic music, the partners face each other and begin moving to the beat of the music; the student in the middle of the classroom creates his own "dance" using the broom as a "partner."
4. When you abruptly turn down the volume of the recording, all of the students are to quickly exchange partners.
5. Following this mad scramble, the student left without a partner is required to dance with the broom in the center of the classroom.
6. Turn up the volume and the activity continues until a number of students have been given the opportunity to "boogie" with the witch's broom.
7. Types of recordings suggested for this activity include the following:

   Various selections of rhythmic, current popular music

   Instrumental recordings for creative movement, motor skills development, and physical fitness

   Selections of music for gymnastics, floor exercises, rope jumping, and parachute play

4

THANKSGIVING

Fourth Thursday in November

Little did the Pilgrims realize what they started when they invited their Indian friends to Plymouth Colony in 1621 for a feast of thanksgiving. What began as a humble offering of thanks to God for surviving a severe winter and enjoying an abundant harvest of crops has evolved into that grand American holiday we celebrate each November. How we celebrate! We have a lavish turkey dinner with all the trimmings; Macy's Thanksgiving Day Parade; the football game on television. All of these are familiar expressions of our present-day observance of Thanksgiving, expressions that often overshadow the remembrance of the historical incident from which the holiday originated. An excellent method for directing your students' attention to the events surrounding that first Thanksgiving is the application of music to your classroom holiday preparations. The musical activities in the pages immediately following are designed to assist you and your class in commemorating the original American harvest home.

The Pilgrims' arduous voyage across the Atlantic Ocean is recalled in "Mayflower Mural," a project for visually representing the contrasting moods of various musical compositions. "Pilgrim-Indian 'Get Acquainted' Dance," a funky, rhythmic rendition of the first meeting of the settlers from England and the native Americans, underscores the spirit of friendship and cooperation characteristic of the occasion. "Turkey" is a modern interpretation of the "after dinner entertainment" known to have amused the Pilgrims and their Indian guests—a rousing card game for learning to identify common musical symbols. "Indian Feather Fest," a lively movement activity, blends the properties of rhythm and pantomime. The "'Horn' of Plenty," symbolic of the first Thanksgiving, is a fitting musical adaptation of the traditional harvest cornucopia.

To include music in your class's preparation for Thanksgiving is to increase the students' awareness of that festive autumn happening of long ago. So, don't be content merely to lead a group discussion on the origins of the holiday or lecture your students from the text of a history book. Turn the youngsters on to eager involvement by including one or more musical activities in your holiday plans. Successful results are certain to follow, for music is an exciting, practical means for motivating your students to recognize and appreciate their genuinely American Thanksgiving heritage.

"HORN" OF PLENTY
Bulletin Board Idea

Objective: To develop familiarity with various songs that are associated with a particular subject.

Grades: 2 – 4

1. Prepare for this activity by covering the bulletin board with plain background paper.

2. Enlarge the following French horn illustration and draw the instrument on the background (The horn need not be drawn in extensive detail; the general shape of the instrument and a few characteristic features are all that are necessary):

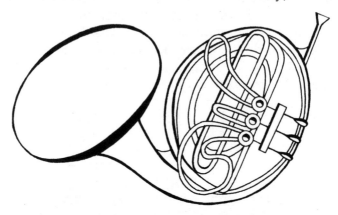

3. Give each student crayons and/or colored pencils, glue or paste, scraps of colored construction paper, and scissors.

4. Explain to the students that the Thanksgiving cornucopia or "horn of plenty" is the traditional symbol of abundance; show the class a picture of the cornucopia and tell the students that they will be designing a "musical" horn of plenty.

5. Ask the class to name as many song titles as they can that deal with Thanksgiving, Pilgrims, Indians, autumn, harvest, peace, sharing, friendship, feasting, etc. The students may scan their music texts or books in the school library in search of the titles, or they may name those with which they are already familiar; list the titles on the chalkboard.

6. Direct the class to proceed as follows:

   A. To represent the plentiful supply of food flowing from the cornucopia, each student fashions a particular fruit and/or vegetable from the construction paper scraps.

   B. The student then clearly prints one of the song titles listed on the chalkboard on each of the fruits or vegetables. For example, each letter of every word in his selected title may be printed on a kernel of an ear of corn.

7. When all of the fruits and vegetables have been completed, invite the class to attach those items onto the bulletin board. The students, in groups of two or three at a time, attractively arrange and glue the fruits and vegetables in such a way as to suggest that they are tumbling out of the mouth of the French horn.

8. Sample song titles for use in this activity include the following:

   We Gather Together
   Ten Little Indians
   Come, Ye Thankful People, Come
   Over the River and Through the Wood
   Harvest Song
   It's a Small World
   For the Beauty of the Earth
   I'd Like to Teach the World to Sing
   Praise God From Whom All Blessings Flow
   America, the Beautiful
   Grandpa's Turkey
   Now Thank We All Our God
   Corn Grinding Song
   Pilgrims' Chorus
   God Bless America
   Let There Be Peace on Earth

TURKEY

Game

Objective: To develop the ability to recognize various musical symbols.

Grades: 4 – 6 (six - eight players)

   1. Prepare one deck of game cards as follows:

     A. Cut twenty-six 4″ × 6″ unlined index cards in half.

     B. Divide the resulting fifty-two cards into thirteen groups of four cards per group; every card of each group is labeled with one of the following musical symbols:

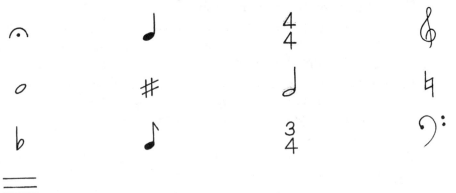

     C. On each card, draw the symbol in two positions as shown:

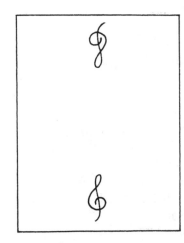

(For durability and to facilitate play, each of the cards may be laminated in plastic.)

2. When the game cards have been prepared, gather together enough tablespoons for *one less than the total number of players.*

3. Arrange the spoons in a row in the center of a table as shown:

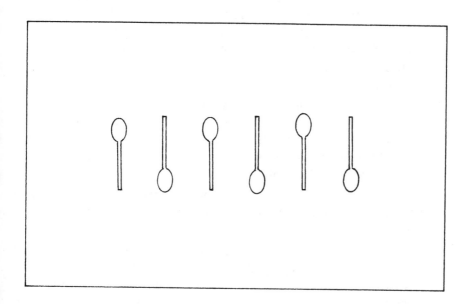

4. Direct the students who will play the game to sit in chairs around the table; the players are to be spaced evenly from one another and within reach of the row of spoons.

5. Select one student to be the scorekeeper; he prints the name of each player on a sheet of paper.

6. Another student, chosen to be the dealer, shuffles the deck and deals three musical symbol cards to each player; he places the pile of remaining cards face down on the table in front of him.

7. To begin the game, the dealer draws the top card from the deck. If the musical symbol on that card matches one of the symbols on a card already in his hand, he keeps that particular card; if the card drawn does not match one of those in his hand, he passes it (or any other non-matching card in his possession) face down to the player on his right. (To pass the card, the dealer *slides* it against the table top.)

8. The player on the dealer's right then picks up the card passed to him. If it matches one of those in his hand, he keeps that card; if it does not match, he passes that card or another non-matching card to the player on *his* right by sliding it face down against the table top.

9. As they receive cards from the left and pass them to the right, all the players move their cards *at the same time*, matching identical symbols and discarding those that do not match. (Having initiated the passing, the dealer continues drawing from the top of the deck and maintains the counterclockwise movement of the cards.)

10. The passing of the cards continues until one of the players accumulates three musical symbols of the same kind. The moment he discovers that he is holding three identical symbols, that player reaches for one of the spoons and places it directly in front of him on the table.

11. As soon as the other players realize that a spoon has been removed from the center of the table, they all frantically grab for the remaining spoons.

12. Following a moment of pandemonium, one player is left without a spoon. He has thus "lost" that round of play, and underneath his name on the scoresheet, the scorekeeper prints the letter "T." Each time a round of play is lost, an additional letter is written below the losing student's name until the word T-U-R-K-E-Y has been spelled. Then, the player is declared to be "out," and for him the game is over.

13. The game begins again as described above, this time with one less player and one less spoon. Eventually, all but one of the "turkeys" are eliminated; that partciular student is declared to be the winner of the game.

14. Additional game suggestions include the following:

    A. For best results, a minimum of four students is required to begin playing the game. The maximum number should be ten players.

    B. The players should be encouraged to glance at the received cards *briefly* and pass them on *quickly*. Card pileups between players may occur, but they need not be a problem; the student merely reaches for a card from his left whether it rests by itself or in a pile of cards.

C. Plastic spoons may be used in the game; however, if they splinter or break, they are to be replaced immediately.

D. For obvious reasons, knives and/or forks should *never* be substituted for spoons in playing the game.

MAYFLOWER MURAL

Project

Objective: To develop an awareness of the ability of music to describe various moods.

Grades: 1 – 3

1. Enlarge the following illustration of the Pilgrims' ship, the Mayflower, on the chalkboard (you need not draw the ship in extensive detail; the general shape of the ship and a few characteristic features are all that are necessary):

2. Give each student crayons, scissors, and a large sheet of drawing paper.

3. Direct the student to fold his sheet of paper in half widthwise; he

then opens the sheet which is divided into two sections by the fold line.

4. At the bottom of one of the sections, each student is to print the phrase "A good day"; at the bottom of the other, "A bad day."

5. Using the illustration on the board as a model, the student is to sketch a picture of the Mayflower in *each* section of the drawing paper.

6. Direct the class to proceed as follows:

   A. As you play a recording of bright, pleasant-sounding music, each student is to complete the appropriately labeled Mayflower picture by adding various touches to create a positive, agreeable atmosphere. For example, to show "a good day" on the Pilgrims' voyage across the Atlantic Ocean, light, frothy waves may be drawn lapping at the ship's hull as the gently billowing sails are silhouetted against a blazing blue, cloudless sky.

   B. When the first Mayflower picture has been finished, the student then transforms the ship in the other section of his sheet into the total opposite of the first. As you play a recording of threatening, angry-sounding music, each student adds specific effects to create a negative, uneasy scene. For example, in showing "a bad day" aboard the Mayflower, the ship's sails may be tattered by the gusty winds of an ocean storm, and enormous waves may be illustrated crashing onto the Mayflower's deck while jagged bolts of lightning slash across a thick, gray sky.

7. When both Mayflower scenes have been completed, instruct the class to carefully cut along the fold line of the paper, separating the drawings.

8. Collect all of the illustrations. Tape together the "good day" Mayflower scenes side by side onto the wall to form a mural; attach and display the "bad day" drawings in the same manner.

9. Suggested musical compositions for this activity include the following:

Good Day	**Bad Day**
"En Bateau" (In a Boat) from *Petite Suite* – Debussy	Overture to *Der fliegende Hollander* (The Flying Dutchman),

Good Day	Bad Day
"Shaker Tune" (Theme and Variations on "Simple Gifts") from *Appalachian Spring* –Copland	Opening section – Wagner *Scheherazade*, Op. 35, Fourth Movement (Section entitled "The Ship Goes to Pieces on a Rock Surmounted by a Bronze Warrior") – Rimsky-Korsakov
"Song of the Bell Buoy" from *Harbor Vignettes* – Donaldson	A Ground – Handel
"Polovetsian Dances" from *Prince Igor*, First section – Borodin	"Fog and Storm" from *Harbor Vignettes* – Donaldson

PILGRIM–INDIAN "GET ACQUAINTED" DANCE
Rhythmic Activity

Objective: To develop the ability to use body movements to describe various action words.

Grades: K – 6

1. Prepare *two* sets of unlined index cards (each set contains enough cards for *half* the members of the class) as follows:

   A. Each card for Group 1—the Pilgrims—is numbered with a *black* numeral in the upper right corner and is labeled with one of the following action words:

Stamp	Shuffle	Stumble
Blink	Clap	Skip
Flap	Bounce	Wiggle
Jump	Nod	Hop
Sway	Stoop	Sniffle

   B. Each card for Group 2—the Indians—is numbered with a *red* numeral in the upper right corner and is labeled with one of the following action words:

Strut	Giggle	Stretch
Shake	Twist	Twitch
Scramble	Crawl	Wave
Roll	Walk	Slide
Spin	Step	Leap

2. Divide the students into two groups which are separated at opposite ends of the classroom. Provide each group member with

one of the above prepared cards. The Pilgrims receive the action word cards numbered with the *black* numerals; the Indians receive the cards with the *red* numerals.

3. Upon a given signal, the members of each group are to scatter and locate their "partners" in the other group. For example, the Pilgrim holding the card labeled with the *black* number "five" is to find the Indian who has possession of the card marked with the *red* number "five."

4. When the student partners have found one another, they separate into pairs around the classroom.

5. Each pair of students reads the words on their cards and begins planning a "get acquainted dance," combining the names of and the motions suggested by the individual action words. For example, when the Pilgrim holding the "stamp" card finds his Indian partner who may have possession of the "strut" card, the two students together invent an original pattern of rhythmic motions named either "The Stamp-Strut" or "The Strut-Stamp"; both the prancing steps of the "strut" and the heavy foot movements of the "stamp"are to be incorporated into the dance.

6. After several minutes of preparation and rehearsal, direct the students to perform their dances to the beat of a recording of bouncy, rhythmic music that you play. (If desired, you may ask for volunteer student partners to perform their dances for the class; a guessing game may then ensue as the students attempt to discover the name of each pair's dance by carefully watching the gestures of the partners.)

7. In order to encourage more action word combinations resulting in additional "get acquainted dances," the activity may proceed in one of the following manners:

   A. When the action word cards have been distributed, tell the Pilgrims holding even-numbered cards to select Indian partners with even-numbered cards; odd-numbered cards with odd-numbered cards.

   B. Tell the Pilgrims holding even-numbered cards to select Indian partners with odd-numbered cards; odd-numbered cards with even-numbered cards.

   C. Following the first round of the activity, collect the cards from each group, shuffle, and redistribute them to the students; direct each group member (now holding a different card) to locate his partner according to one of the above methods.

8. To accommodate younger students, you may facilitate this activity by pinning numbered tags onto the shirts of the students; then whisper a particular action word to each student and the activity proceeds as described above.

9. Types of recordings suggested for this activity include the following:

   Various selections of rhythmic, current popular music

   Instrumental recordings for creative movement, motor skills development, and physical fitness

   Selections of music for gymnastics, floor exercises, rope jumping, and parachute play

INDIAN FEATHER FEST

Pantomime

Objective: To develop the ability to use body movements to describe familiar activities.

Grades: K – 3

1. Enlarge the following, and, using it as a pattern, cut out enough feather shapes from colored construction paper for the members of the class:

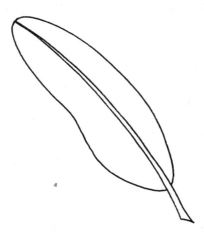

2. On one side of each feather, print a particular pantomime situation; each situation describes a specific Thanksgiving-related activity. For example:

A Pretend you are carving the Thanksgiving turkey.

B. Pretend you are eating Thanksgiving dinner.

C. Pretend you are sitting in church.

D. Pretend you are shopping for groceries for the Thanksgiving dinner.

E. Pretend you are watching the Thanksgiving Day Parade on television.

F. Pretend you are washing the dishes after the Thanksgiving meal.

G. Pretend you are stuffing the Thanksgiving turkey.

H. Pretend you are saying grace at the dinner table.

I. Pretend you are watching a football game on television.

J. Pretend you are making a pumpkin pie.

K. Pretend you are calling your relatives on the telephone to invite them for Thanksgiving dinner.

L. Pretend you are helping Mom clean the house before the dinner guests arrive.

M. Pretend you and your family are boarding a plane to visit Grandma's house for Thanksgiving Day.

N. Pretend you are setting the table for Thanksgiving dinner.

O. Pretend you are greeting your dinner guests at the front door.

P. Pretend you are walking into Grandma's house, and you smell the delicious meal that is cooking.

Q. Pretend you are beginning to write your Christmas gift list.

3. Tape a toothpick to the base of each feather and then insert the feathers with attached picks into a large ball of modeling clay. (The printed sides of the feathers are to face the center of the arrangement so that the pantomime scenes are not readily visible to the students.)

4. Set the feather centerpiece in the middle of the floor, and direct the students to form a large circle around the classroom; each student is to stand so he is not touching his neighbor.

5. Inform the class that, as you play a steady rhythmic pattern on a hand drum or similar sound-producing device, they are to begin walking around the circle to the beat of the drum.

6. As you tap out the rhythm, call out the name of one of the students; this is the signal for that particular student to leave the

circle of his classmates, rhythmically move to the centerpiece, and withdraw a feather.

7. That student then reads, in secret, the pantomime instructions printed on his feather as he rhythmically moves back to his place in the circle and resumes walking to the beat with his classmates.

8. When every member of the class has obtained a feather, stop the rhythmic drum beat and tell the students to scatter around the room.

9. As you play a recording of appropriate music, direct the students to pantomime those activities printed on their feathers.

10. Call upon various students to demonstrate their pantomimes for the class who are to determine the Thanksgiving situations described by carefully watching the gestures of their classmates.

11. To accommodate younger students, you may facilitate this activity by whispering the particular pantomime instructions to each student after he has selected a feather; the activity then continues as described above.

12. Suitable musical compositions for this activity include the following:

"Wheat Dance" from *Estancia* – Ginastera

Sonata No. 8 in C Minor, Op. 13, ("Pathétique"), Second Movement (Adagio cantabile) – Beethoven

"The White Peacock" from *Roman Sketches*, Op. 7, No. 1 – Griffes

Various additional compositions of instrumental music for interpretative movement, pantomime, and ballet

5

CHRISTMAS

December 25

Christmas is a holiday for the senses—the silent twinkling of tiny lights illuminating soft pine trees; the warm, "down-home" smells of baking cookies and yeast breads; the buzzing crowds of package-laden shoppers hustling through the aisles of tinsel-decorated department stores. But the most universal herald of the Christmas season is echoed in the familiar strains of the traditional holiday songs and carols. From the simple refrains of "Up on the Housetop" to the magnificent choruses of Handel's *Messiah*, the wealth of special Christmas music is the perfect foundation on which you and your students may prepare for this most cherished of holidays. Thus, this chapter presents a collection of merry classroom activities centered around those best-loved holiday tunes.

"Christmas Gift Potpourri," for example, is a splendid activity for familiarizing the students with the words of a particular holiday song while inspiring them to compose a set of original lyrics. Learning the words of the carols becomes an engaging beanbag game in "Holiday Song Toss-Across," and "Holiday 'Ear Words,'" a spirited physical response experience, sharpens the students' listening skills through the use of familiar Christmas songs. The musical concept of line and space notes is featured in the boisterous team competition, "Christmas

Stocking Relay," and in "Holiday Notes," the students become acquainted with conventional musical notation while exercising their artistic abilities. A Yuletide classic, *The Nutcracker Suite*, is explored as the students construct festive "Musical Wreaths." "The Christmas Bounce" is an adventure in synchronized rhythmic movement that may be rehearsed for a classroom holiday performance. In observance of the celebration of Hanukkah, two special entries are included in this chapter for commemorating the Jewish "Festival of Lights." Although the chapter's Christmas activities are designed for easy adaptation to the Jewish holiday, "Musical Candles" is a spunky seek-and-find game for learning to recognize common musical symbols, and "Musical Menorah Greeting Cards" serves as a unique visual introduction to the concept of the musical scale.

Christmas is a marvelous blend of fond memories and joyful anticipation, whispered secrets and sentimental dreams. And the elegant gift-wrapping on this many-faceted Christmas package is the abundance of traditional holiday music. Therefore, share the magic of music with your students as you plan your class's celebration of this jubilant occasion. No other holiday is graced with such a natural bounty of carols and songs, and to actively participate in all aspects of that music is to experience Christmas at its fullest. For you and your students, make it a season "to be jolly."

CHRISTMAS GIFT POTPOURRI
Bulletin Board Idea

Objective: To develop familiarity with a particular holiday song.

Grades: 3 – 6

1. Prepare for this activity by covering the bulletin board with plain background paper.
2. Design the background as follows:
   A. Using cutout alphabet letters, spell "The Twelve Days of Christmas" across the top of the bulletin board.

   B. Draw a vertical line with a dark-colored marking pen from underneath the words to the bottom of the board, dividing the background in half.

   C. Directly below the letters on the left half of the board, spell the word "Then"; on the right side, "Now."

   D. Divide the remaining area of *each* half of the background into twelve approximately equal sections.

3. Give each student crayons or oil-based pastel crayons.

4. Explain to the class that "The Twelve Days of Christmas" is an old English folk carol which describes a particular custom of holiday gift-giving; write the words of the song on the chalkboard, underlining the various gifts denoted in the lyrics as follows:

On the first day of Christmas my true love sent to me a partridge in a pear tree.

On the second day of Christmas my true love sent to me two turtle doves.

On the third day of Christmas my true love sent to me three French hens.

On the fourth day of Christmas my true love sent to me four calling (or colly) birds.

On the fifth day of Christmas my true love sent to me five golden rings.

On the sixth day of Christmas my true love sent to me six geese a-laying.

On the seventh day of Christmas my true love sent to me seven swans a-swimming.

On the eighth day of Christmas my true love sent to me eight maids a-milking.

On the ninth day of Christmas my true love sent to me nine ladies dancing.

On the tenth day of Christmas my true love sent to me ten lords a-leaping.

On the eleventh day of Christmas my true love sent to me eleven pipers piping.

On the twelfth day of Christmas my true love sent to me twelve drummers drumming.

5. Select various students to neatly print the names of the under-lined gift items in the twelve sections of the "Then" side of the bulletin board—on the *left* half of the background. ("A partridge in a pear tree" is lettered with dark-colored crayons at the top of one of the sections; in the adjoining space, "Two turtle doves;" in the next section, "Three French hens;" etc.)

6. Then ask the students to name as many modern Christmas gift items as they can, and list them on the chalkboard; for example, dolls, skates, bicycles, etc.

7. Maintaining the number and pattern of syllables in each line of "The Twelve Days of Christmas" the students substitute the gifts designated in the original song with the suggested contemporary gift items; the names of these "Now" gifts are clearly printed as labels for the sections of the *right* side of the bulletin board. Sample modern gift items include the following:

A wide-screen color T.V.

Two ten-speed bikes

Three tape decks

Four roller skates

Five Barbie dolls

Six record albums
Seven football helmets
Eight gold pierced earrings
Nine tennis racquets
Ten calculators
Eleven pairs of blue jeans
Twelve furry kittens

8. As you play a recording of "The Twelve Days of Christmas," invite the class to complete the bulletin board scene. In groups of two or three at a time, the students attractively illustrate the "Then" and "Now" gift items with crayons in the twenty-four sections of the background beneath each gift name.

HOLIDAY NOTES

Bulletin Board Idea

Objective: To develop an awareness of conventional musical notation.

Grades: 3 – 6

1. Prepare for this activity by covering the bulletin board with plain background paper.

2. Select a familiar Christmas carol[1] from a music text or book in the school library. With a dark-colored marking pen, draw a portion of that song (including the title and lyrics) on the background. For example:

DECK THE HALLS

Deck the halls with boughs of hol-ly,   Fa, la, la, la, la,   la,   la,   la, la

3. Give each student crayons and/or colored pencils, scissors, glue or paste, and scraps of colored construction paper.

4. From the paper scraps, each student is to fashion a particular Christmas symbol—e.g., a stocking, ornament, pine tree, snowflake, angel, gift-wrapped package, wreath, snowman, star, bell,

---

[1]If the chosen musical example is printed with more than one note in vertical alignment over each syllable of the words, copy *only the top notes*—melody—of the song.

etc. The symbol is to be made a bit larger than the oval portion of each musical note drawn on the bulletin board; inform the class of this size requirement as they design their holiday objects.

5. When the Christmas symbols have been completed, the students carefully cut them out with scissors.

6. In groups of two or three at a time, invite the students to attach their holiday objects directly onto the oval portions of the notes on the background. When covered with the colorful paper symbols, the notes of the song appear to be created from the various Christmas decorations.

7. If desired, other festive touches may be added to the scene: the vertical bar lines ▤ might be made into red-and-white peppermint sticks; the treble clef 𝄞 may be curled into a bright Christmas ribbon; the time signature 4 might be designed as frosted gingerbread cookies, etc.

8. To celebrate Hanukkah, this activity may be conducted in the above manner substituting a traditional Hebrew tune for the Christmas song. The musical notes are then formed from appropriate holiday symbols such as candles, dreidels, Stars of David, menorahs, crowns, etc.

CHRISTMAS STOCKING RELAY

Game

Objective: To develop the ability to distinguish between "line" and "space" musical notes.

Grades: 1 – 3 (entire class participation)

1. Prepare *two* Christmas stockings as follows:

   A. Draw each stocking approximately eighteen inches in height. Cut one out of red construction paper and one out of green construction paper.

   B. On each stocking, draw enough "line" and "space" musical notes for *half* the members of the class. Both stockings are designed with the *same notes* in the *same vertical arrangement* as shown in this example:

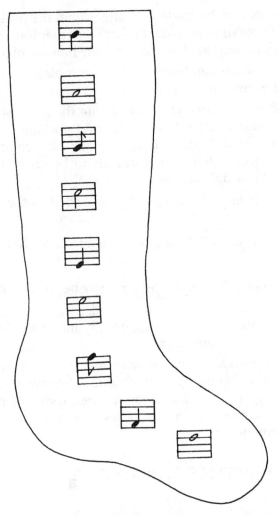

2. When the two stockings have been completed, draw the following musical staff and notes[2] on the chalkboard:

---

[2]The difference between line and space notes is determined exclusively by the
placement of the *oval portions* of the notes on the staff. The stems, flags, and whether or
not the notes are filled in are irrelevant to that distinction.

3. Explain to the class that musical notes are classified as either "line" notes or "space" notes. If the oval portion of the note is situated *on* a line of the staff, that note is identified as a "line" note ; if the note is situated *between* two lines, it is designated as a "space" note . (On the above chalkboard illustration, the first, third, and fifth notes are line notes; the second, fourth, and sixth notes are space notes.)

4. In order to reinforce the concept of line-space notes, draw several additional note examples on the chalkboard for the class to identify.

5. When the students appear to be fairly proficient at differentiating between line and space notes, divide the class into two teams.

6. Direct the team members to form two lines and kneel down on the floor at opposite ends of the classroom; give each student a pencil.

7. Instruct the class how to play the game as follows:

   A. Give the first student in each team line one of the prepared stockings which he places face down on the floor in front of him. (Each team receives a stocking of a different color—Team A is given the red stocking; Team B, the green stocking.)

   B. Upon a given signal, that student turns the stocking over and identifies the first note example (drawn near the cuff of the stocking). If it is a line note, he prints an "L" beneath the example; if it is a space note, he writes an "S."

   C. The first student then passes the stocking to the student next to him and stands up in line.

   D. The second student identifies and correctly marks the second example on the list, and he also stands.

   E. The stocking is passed on to each successive student until all of the line-space notes have been properly labeled (from cuff to toe) and the team members are standing in their line. The winner of the relay is the team that first *correctly* completes the line-space identification of all the muscial notes on the stocking.

   F. Following a considerable amount of noisy excitement, clarification becomes necessary. To ensure that the teams have indeed accurately marked the line-space notes, declare the "official" winner *after examining both stockings for errors.*

G. If you discover an error(s) on only one of the stockings, the team whose stocking is error-free is announced to be the winner. If both teams produce stockings with errors, return them to the respective student groups who must locate and *correct* the error(s). The first team to do so is declared to be the winner of the relay.

8. To lengthen the game by providing additional opportunities for the students to identify line-space notes, prepare several stockings for use by each team. Thus, extra rounds of the relay might be played.

MUSICAL CANDLES

Game

Objective: To develop the ability to recognize various musical symbols.

Grades: K – 3 (entire class participation)

1. Prepare *two* sets of colored construction paper cards as follows:

    A. Set 1 is composed of enough rectangular-shaped "candlesticks" for *half* the members of the class. One of the following musical symbols is drawn on each stick:

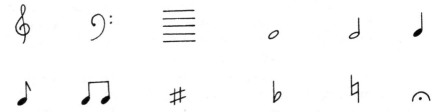

    B. Set 2 is composed of enough oval-shaped "flames" for *half* the members of the class. Each flame is labeled with one of the above musical symbols.

2. Divide the students into two groups; each group is to form a large circle at opposite ends of the classroom.

3. Distribute the prepared cards to the students. Give the candlesticks to each member of one of the circles; the flames to the students of the other circle.

4. Direct the students to hold their cards and begin walking around the circles to the beat of a recording of bouncy, rhythmic music that you will play.

5. After a few moments, abruptly turn down the volume of the recording; this is the signal for each member of both circles to dash across the classroom and locate his "partner" who holds the card labeled with the same musical symbol. For example, the

student holding the candlestick on which is drawn the ♩ must find his partner who has possession of the flame labeled with

the ♩.

6. When the partners have found one another, they are to immediately sit down on the floor.

7. The last pair of students to locate each other and sit on the floor are declared to be "out" for that round of the activity; they are to join their candlestick and flame together and attach it to the bulletin board, window, or other designated area of the classroom.

8. The activity then continues as the remaining students return to their respective circles and proceed their rhythmic walking to the beat of the music as you turn the volume up once again.

9. The partners who successfully match their symbols for every round of the activity without being eliminated are declared to be the "Musical Candle Champions"; those two students then join their candlestick and flame together, you attach a colored paper candleholder to the base, and the champions' candle is displayed prominently among the others in the classroom.

10. Types of recordings suggested for this activity include the following:

Selected bouncy, lively holiday music—e.g., *Hava Nagila*

Various selections of rhythmic, current popular music

Instrumental recordings for creative movement, motor skills development, and physical fitness

Selections of music for gymnastics, floor exercises, rope jumping, and parachute play

HOLIDAY "EAR WORDS"
Game

Objective: To develop the ability to listen for particular words.

Grades: K – 3 (entire class participation)

1. Select a holiday song that contains a specific recurring word(s) in the lyrics. For example:

   O Christmas tree, O Christmas tree,
   Your branches green delight us.
   O Christmas tree, O Christmas tree,
   Your branches green delight us.
   They're green when summer days are bright.
   They're green when winter snow is white.
   O Christmas tree, O Christmas tree,
   Your branches green delight us.

2. Explain that, as you play a vocal recording of the song, the students are to respond in a certain manner when a particular word is heard. For example, using the above lyrics, tell the class that each time the word "tree" is sung, they are to quickly stand up and then sit down.

3. Choose another "ear word" and play the recording a second time. An additional motion is added to the first—in the example above, the word "green" might indicate that the students are to stand up, spin around once, and sit down again.

4. Select a third word and play the recording once more, adding yet another movement to the students' performance. For example, whenever the word "Christmas" is heard, the students must place both hands on top of their heads.

5. The activity continues until the students are accurately responding to the designated "ear words" of the holiday song.

6. Holiday songs suggested for use in this activity include the following:

   Christmas
   The Twelve Days of Christmas
   We Wish You a Merry Christmas
   Rudolph, the Red-Nosed Reindeer
   Jingle Bells
   Winter Wonderland
   Silver Bells

   Hanukkah
   In the Window
   I Have a Little Dreidel
   Shalom Chaverim

HOLIDAY SONG TOSS-ACROSS
Game

Objective: To develop familiarity with various holiday songs.

Grades: K – 6 (entire class participation)

In preparation for this activity, construct a beanbag in the shape of a familiar holiday object—a bell, star, or ornament for Christmas; a dreidel or crown for Hanukkah.

1. Select a particular holiday song and write a verse[3] of that tune on the chalkboard. For example:

   Dashing through the snow in a one-horse open sleigh,
   O'er the fields we go, laughing all the way.
   Bells on bobtail ring, making spirits bright.
   What fun it is to ride and sing a sleighing song tonight.
   Jingle bells, jingle bells, jingle all the way.
   Oh, what fun it is to ride in a one-horse open sleigh.
   Jingle bells, jingle bells, jingle all the way.
   Oh, what fun it is to ride in a one-horse open sleigh.

2. With the class, listen to a recording of the song and chant the words over and over until the students appear to be fairly proficient at reciting them.

3. Have the class sit in a large circle on the floor; choose one student to hold the prepared beanbag.

4. Upon a given signal, the student holding of the beanbag recites the opening phrase of the holiday song—"Dashing through the snow ... "

5. He then randomly tosses the beanbag across the circle of students. The classmate who catches the bag must respond by correctly chanting the second phrase of the lyrics— "... in a one-horse open sleigh ... "

6. That student tosses the beanbag to a third classmate who, in turn, must accurately call out the next phrase of the song. The procedure is repeated for each successive phrase of the verse.

7. If a student does not call out the correct phrase or fails to respond within a reasonable amount of time, that student must sit down

---

[3]For the purposes of this activity, the term "verse" has been expanded to include the chorus or refrain as well as the stanza.

on the floor in the center of the circle (until he is replaced by the next erring classmate). The beanbag is then given to another student who begins the activity over again by reciting the opening phrase of the song.

8. The tossing of the beanbag proceeds for several rounds until the entire verse has been successfully chanted without any errors. Then, choose another holiday song and repeat the activity as described above.

MUSICAL WREATHS

Project

Objective: To develop familiarity with a classic composition of musical literature.

Grades: 3 – 6

1. Enlarge the following pattern, make copies of it, and distribute one to each member of the class:

2. Give each student a pencil, crayons and/or colored pencils, scissors, glue or paste, and two large sheets of colored construction paper—one, white; the other, red.

3. On the chalkboard, place the name of the musical composition (and the composer) to which the students will be listening:

   The Nutcracker Suite – Tchaikovsky

4. Tell the story of *The Nutcracker*[4] to the class as follows:

   There once lived a little girl named Marie. At a Christmas party, she received a wooden nutcracker in the shape of a man. After she went to bed that night, Marie dreamed that she was walking into the living room to get the nutcracker. To her surprise, she found the toys all dancing happily underneath the Christmas tree. Suddenly, an army of mice led by the mouse king attacked the frolicking toys; the nutcracker was placed in a dangerous predicament. Quickly removing one of her slippers, Marie hurled it at the mouse king and rescued the little nutcracker. To her amazement, the nutcracker turned into a handsome prince, who, in gratitude, took Marie to the magical Land of the Sugar Plum Fairy where a fantastic display was presented by all the dancing toys.

5. Explain to the students that they will be making Christmas wreaths that illustrate the sequence of events in the musical composition, *The Nutcracker Suite*.

6. Tell the class that the greater portion of the musical composition—i.e., the ballet—is descriptive of the dream sequence of the story, and list on the chalkboard the eight scenes that will be part of each wreath:

   Overture
   March
   Dance of the Sugar Plum Fairy
   Dance of the Russian Dolls
   Arabian Dance
   Chinese Dance
   Dance of the Toy Flutes
   Waltz of the Flowers

---

[4]This version of *The Nutcracker* has been compiled from several interpretations of the story. Specific details may vary from source to source.

7. Direct the class to proceed as follows:

A. Each student carefully cuts out the pattern given to him.

B. He folds the sheet of white construction paper in half widthwise and places the dotted lines of the pattern against the fold; he traces around the inside and outside edges of the pattern with a pencil.

C. The student then cuts out the traced pattern through the double thickness of construction paper along the solid lines as shown:

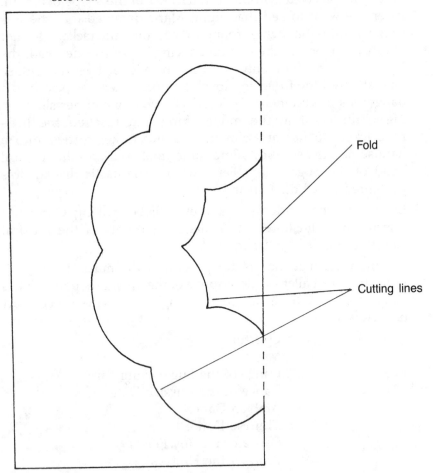

Fold

Cutting lines

D. He opens up the construction paper cutout to reveal a "wreath" of eight segments, each of which he outlines with a dark-colored crayon as indicated:

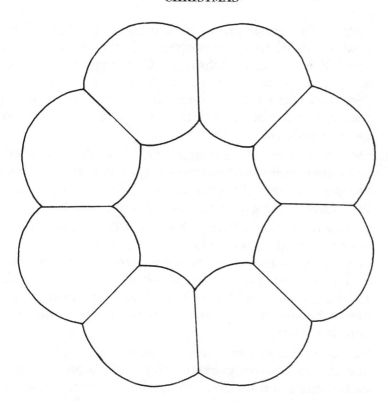

8. Tell the students that, as they listen to a recording of *The Nutcracker Suite*, they are to appropriately illustrate the various scenes described in the musical composition and listed on the chalkboard. One scene is to be designed in each section of the wreath, and the sequence of the scenes is to proceed in a *clockwise arrangement* around the wreath—regardless of the segment in which the student chooses to draw the "Overture" scene, the "March" is to be illustrated in the section that adjoins in a clockwise direction.

9. As the students work on their individual wreath projects, you should guide them in designing appropriate illustrations for the eight scenes by pointing out the various events as they occur and are depicted in the music. Thus, the following musical descriptions and suggested drawings to accompany the individual selections are included:

A. "Overture" – The stringed instruments announce the first melody followed by swiftly moving patterns played by the clarinets and flutes. A second theme is then sounded by the violins. The music grows with excitement as the overture creates a light, happy atmosphere for the remaining events that follow. A scene featuring a Christmas motif would be most appropriate for the first section of the wreath. A gaily decorated Christmas tree surrounded by brightly wrapped packages would be most suitable in setting a festive mood for the remainder of the composition.

B. "March" – The majestic march tune initially played by the brass instruments and clarinets suggests the formal arrival of the guests at the Christmas party. They enter, dressed in all their finery, and gather around the Christmas tree.

C. "Dance of the Sugar Plum Fairy" – The delicate sounds of the celesta[5] prevail in this first section of the dream sequence. In her dream, Marie imagines a land where toys come to life under the spell of the Sugar Plum Fairy. Flitting among dolls, stuffed animals, and toy soldiers, the tiny pixie touches each one with her magic wand to make them come alive to entertain Marie.

D. "Dance of the Russian Dolls" – Topped with tall, furry hats and clad in peasant garments and shiny boots, the Russian dolls dance at a frantic pace to the sounds of the full orchestra punctuated by the shaking of a tambourine. With their arms folded across their chests, these dancers squat close to the floor and kick out their legs in rhythm to the rapid music.

E. "Arabian Dance" – The lovely Arabian dolls dance to an exotic, quiet melody first played by the reed instruments, then answered by the violins. Flowing chiffon veils and delicate filigree jewelry adorn the dancers as they gracefully move to the smooth music.

F. "Chinese Dance" – The flutes and piccolos are heard above a strong rhythmic pattern played by the bassoon, which characterizes the dance of the Chinese dolls. Dressed in flowing pajama-like garments and flat-brimmed coolie hats, the dancers from the Orient keep up a vigorous pace.

G. "Dance of the Toy Flutes" – The toy flutes take center stage having been animated by the Sugar Plum Fairy. The thin, silvery little instruments not only help provide the music to which the other toys move, but they themselves perform their

---

[5]Celesta – a percussion instrument consisting of tuned steel bars connected to a keyboard.

own melody and then strike up a handsome dance as the brass instruments accompany them.

H. "Waltz of the Flowers" – The concluding section of *The Nutcracker Suite* culminates in a vibrant waltz of all the garden flowers in the Land of the Sugar Plum Fairy. Following an introduction featuring the harp, a tune played by the French horns and answered by the clarinets is heard. A sweeping melody sounded by the strings enters next, and, closing one's eyes, it is easy to imagine the vividly colored petals swirling and pirouetting to the full strains of the lavish dance.

10. After the scene wreaths have been completed, each student fashions a "ribbon" from the sheet of red construction paper; he attaches and labels the ribbon as shown:

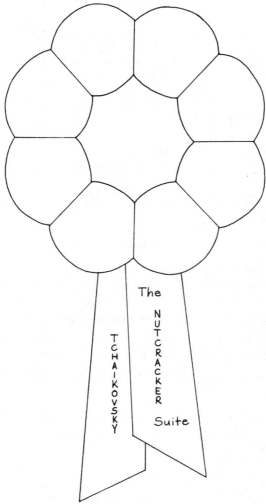

11. To conclude the activity, play the recording once again; the students now follow the story of *The Nutcracker Suite* visually from the sequence of events illustrated on their musical wreaths.

MUSICAL MENORAH GREETING CARDS
Project

Objective: To develop an awareness of the concept of the musical scale.

Grades: 2 – 4

1. On the chalkboard, enlarge the following illustration of a menorah:

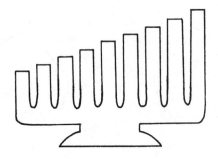

2. Give each student crayons and/or colored pencils and one large sheet of drawing paper.

3. Explain to the class the meaning and significance of the menorah:

The nine-branched candelabrum or menorah is a traditional symbol of the Jewish holiday, Hanukkah (the "Festival of Lights"). To represent the seven-day, eight-night celebration, one more candle is lighted on each successive evening of the observance. The ninth (or tallest) candle in the arrangement, the shammas, is kindled first and then used to light the others.

4. Describe to the students the following characteristics of a musical scale:

A. A scale is a series of *eight* consecutive musical notes that begins and ends on the note of the same name.

B. The notes of a scale are arranged in order of ascending and/or descending pitches.

C. Each scale note is identified by a particular syllable.

5. Write the syllable names of the eight scale notes on the chalkboard and pronounce each one:

Do Re Mi Fa So La Ti Do

6. Direct the class to proceed as follows:

A. Each student is to fold his sheet of drawing paper in half widthwise; this forms a "greeting card" which he places in front of him with the fold to the left.

B. Using the chalkboard illustration as a model, the student designs a Hanukkah menorah on the front of his card.

C. Over every candle the student then draws a flame and prints the appropriate note syllable on each; the flame of the far left candle is labeled "Do"; the flame immediately to the right, "Re"; the next, "Mi"; etc., until all the syllables of the scale are organized in the proper sequence. The shammas flame is designated by the Star of David ✡ .

7. When the "musical menorah" drawings have been completed, assign the class the task of searching through their music texts or books in the school library for traditional Hanukkah songs.

8. After finding an appropriate song, each student then opens his card and prints the words of that song on the inside along with "Happy Hanukkah!" greetings.

9. To conclude the activity and lend a final musical touch to the holiday theme, the students could decorate the remaining areas of their cards with various notes 𝅝 , 𝅗𝅥 , ♩ , ♪.

10. Sample Hanukkah songs for use in this activity include the following:

Hanukkah, Oh, Hanukkah
Joyous Hanukkah
Rock of Ages
Who Can Retell?

THE CHRISTMAS BOUNCE
Rhythmic Activity

Objective: To develop the controlled rhythmic response of bouncing a ball to a particular beat.

Grades: K – 6

1. Give each member of the class one large rubber playground ball. Tell all the students to scatter around the room; each student should stand so he is not touching his neighbor.

2. Tell the class that they will be rehearsing ball-bouncing patterns *without* musical accompaniment until they become fairly proficient at performing the following patterns:

   A. Pattern A

      1. You and the students begin chanting together "one-two-three-four, one-two-three-four," etc. in a steady rhythm.
      2. Holding the ball in front of him with both hands, each student lightly bounces his body up and down to the first four counts of the rhythmic chant, one body-bounce for each number called.
      3. From waist height, he then bounces the ball on the floor and catches it with both hands, one bounce-catch for each of the next four numbers of the chant.
      4. This pattern of alternate body-bouncing (for four counts) and ball-bouncing (for four counts) continues until all the students are simultaneously performing the motions in rhythm with the verbal chant.

   B. Pattern B

      1. Holding the ball in the same position and chanting in the same manner as Pattern A, each student *walks forward* to the first four rhythmic counts, one step for each number called.
      2. He then stops walking and stands in place; from waist height, the student bounces the ball on the floor and catches it with both hands, one bounce-catch for each of the next four numbers of the chant.
      3. This pattern of alternate walking forward (for four counts) and ball-bouncing (for four counts) continues until all the students are simultaneously performing the motions in rhythm with the verbal chant.

C. Pattern C

The same verbal chant is retained, and this set of motions is performed in essentially the same fashion as Pattern B; now, however, each student *walks backward* to the first four counts of the rhythmic chant.

3. Tell the class that you will call out the letters A, B, and C to which the students are to respond by performing the rhythmic motions associated with each—A represents the *body-bouncing* and *ball-bouncing* of Pattern A; B stands for *walking forward* and *ball-bouncing* as in Pattern B; C is representative of *walking backward* and *ball-bouncing*.

4. Call out "A," and the students begin chanting and bouncing that pattern for about thirty seconds. Call out "B," and allow the students a few seconds to get their bearings before beginning that second pattern. Call out "C," permitting a few seconds for recovery, and that pattern is begun.

5. When the students are sufficiently prepared, play a recording of bouncy, rhythmic music that provides the beat for the A, B, and C chanting-bouncing patterns.

6. Variations of this activity include the following:

A. After the class has become successful at performing the above patterns, the verbal chant may be dropped entirely; the students then rhythmically move to the beat of the music alone.

B. For advanced or older students, the rhythmic patterns might be repeated in uninterrupted style as a synchronized class performance. For example, evenly spaced around the room and facing in the same direction, the students proceed from pattern to pattern without the announcement of "A, B, C; A, B, C," etc.

C. Depending on the ability of the particular class, you may add more difficult ball-bouncing routines to the list of patterns. For example, Pattern D might call for bouncing the ball with one hand only; tossing the ball across the front of the body from one hand to the other may be included in Pattern E; Pattern F might require bouncing the ball while assuming a kneeling position, etc.

D. Additional patterns may be created by student partners using one ball for each pair of classmates. (Many interesting and challenging variations are possible for two students performing with one ball—tossing the ball underhand from one partner to the other in rhythm; tossing the ball overhand to each other; bounce-passing the ball from partner to partner, etc.)

7. Types of recordings suggested for this activity include the following:

Selected bouncy, lively holiday music—e.g., *Sleigh Ride, Winter Wonderland, Jingle Bells*

Various selections of rhythmic, current popular music

Instrumental recordings for creative movement, motor skills development, and physical fitness

Selections of music for gymnastics, floor exercises, rope jumping and parachute play

6

VALENTINE'S DAY

February 14

Love and romance are hardly on the minds of elementary school students as they prepare to exchange their valentines with each other on February 14. Rather, Valentine's Day in the elementary classroom presents yet another treasured opportunity for a classroom party. So, having elaborately decorated their valentine boxes with bits of paper lace and cutout heart shapes, the students eagerly await the arrival of the room mothers with their sugary assortment of fancy frosted cookies and multicolored holiday candies. The extent to which music plays a part in the festivities is generally limited to the sound of the pop records that the students bring from home to serve as the party's background music. In fact, music can be a very effective tool for planning a most satisfying classroom observance of Valentine's Day. Through the clever use of the musical activities, games, and projects of this chapter, that annual afternoon spree of gobbling goodies and "getting out of some schoolwork" may be expanded into a truly rewarding midwinter happening.

To develop the students' awareness of the vast amount of music which deals with the Valentine's Day theme, "Musical Candy Hearts" is a stimulating all-class project, and "'My Favorite Things'" results in the construction of a colorful "favorite things" collage as the students learn the lyrics of a particular song. In "Broken Hearts," a fascinating puzzle game, the students exercise their knowledge of musical instrument names, but they must rely solely on their sense of touch for determining the identity of the mysterious "Valentine Box Notes." To provide an opportunity for wiggly bodies to release some pent-up wintertime energy, "Hop-a-Heart" combines rhythmic movement with the holiday motif, and for visualizing the concept of musical steps and skips, "Step-Skip Hearts" is an invigorating team competition. An activity that teaches the students to recognize common musical symbols and their names, "Musical Valentines" encourages the creation of some highly original holiday greetings, and, as a memento of the occasion, each student fashions his own attractive "Musical Mobile" to take home.

The arrival of Valentine's Day is a natural remedy for the long winter blues, and by according music a prominent place in your holiday plans, you and your students can add a fresh, new dimension to the routine classroom preparations. The recipe for a successful holiday celebration calls for a heaping helping of music, whether as a spontaneous rhythmic activity or game at the class party or in advance of the event in the form of innovative greeting cards and decorations. So, as that cheery February fête approaches, let music "be *your* valentine."

MUSICAL CANDY HEARTS

Bulletin Board Idea

Objective: To develop familiarity with various songs that are associated with a particular subject.

Grades: 3 – 6

1. Prepare for this activity by covering the bulletin board with plain background paper.
2. Enlarge the illustration of a candy jar on page 105 and draw the container on the background.
3. On the chalkboard, place the following words:
   Valentine
   Roses
   Heart
   Love
4. Give each student crayons and/or colored pencils, scissors, and one large sheet of red, white, or pink construction paper.

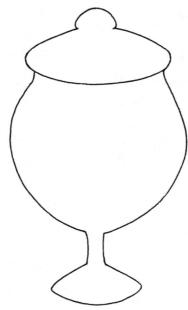

5. Each student is to cut a small valentine shape(s) from the construction paper; he then neatly prints the title of a song that contains one of the above words (or forms of the words) on his heart(s). (The students may scan their music texts or books in the school library in search of the titles, or they may use those with which they are already familiar.)

6. When the song title valentines have been completed, attach them attractively inside the large candy jar on the bulletin board.

7. Although the list of song titles containing the words cited above is virtually endless, a few examples are included here:

My Funny Valentine

The Days of Wine and Roses

Red Roses for a Blue Lady

Moonlight and Roses

My Wild Irish Rose

The Last Rose of Summer

The Yellow Rose of Texas

To a Wild Rose

Heart of Glass

Dear Hearts and Gentle People

Love Me With All Your Heart

Put a Little Love in Your Heart

Zing! Went the Strings of My Heart

Peg O' My Heart

Heartbreaker

It's a Heartache

Dear Heart

Heartbreak Hotel

Heartaches

Heart and Soul

My Heart Belongs to Me

Deep in the Heart of Texas

The Sweetheart Tree

Don't Go Breakin' My Heart

Love Is Blue

An Old-Fashioned Love Song

Love Is a Many-Splendored Thing

I Love You Truly

Love Letters in the Sand

You've Lost That Lovin' Feelin'

Silly Love Songs

I'll Never Fall in Love Again

Can't Help Falling in Love

Let Your Love Follow

Your Love Is Lifting Me Higher

Love Will Keep Us Together

I Loved You Once in Silence

Falling in Love With Love

When You're in Love With a Beautiful Woman

All My Loving

How Deep Is Your Love?

I Want Your Love

Lotta Love

I Honestly Love You

Lookin' for Love

Love Will Find a Way

How Much Love?

World Without Love

If I Loved You

What I Did for Love

All Out of Love

Can't Buy Me Love

Who Loves You?

I Think I Love You

You Made Me Love You

April Love

Goodbye to Love

Never My Love

Love Me Tender

She Loves You

The Things We Do for Love

And I Love Her

"MY FAVORITE THINGS"

Bulletin Board Idea

Objective: To develop familiarity with a particular song.

Grades: 1 – 3

1. Prepare for this activity by covering the bulletin board with plain background paper.

2. With a marking pen, print "My Favorite Things" across the top of the background and draw a *large* valentine beneath the words.

3. Obtain the lyrics of the song "My Favorite Things" from *The Sound of Music* by Rodgers and Hammerstein (either by listening to a recording of the song or by examining a copy of the sheet music); write the words of that song inside the heart shape drawn on the bulletin board background.

4. Give each student scissors, glue or paste, and several magazines to be cut apart.

5. Discuss with the class the meaning of Valentine's Day in the broadest sense—a holiday for remembering persons and things that are liked and/or loved.

6. As you play a recording of "My Favorite Things," the class scans the magazines for pictures, words, and phrases that are representative of those persons and things of which they are fond; the students carefully cut out the items with scissors.

7. Invite the class to attach the magazine cutouts onto the bulletin board. In groups of two or three at a time, the students paste the pictures, words, and phrases around the *outside* of the valentine in attractive overlapping fashion to form a collage of their "favorite things."

BROKEN HEARTS

Game

Objective: To develop familiarity with the names of various musical instruments.

Grades: 4 – 6 (two – six players)

In preparation for this activity, present a brief unit study of various musical instruments to the class.

1. Give each student a pencil, scissors, and a sheet of red or pink construction paper.

2. Folding the paper in half widthwise, each student draws half a valentine shape outward from the folded edge. He cuts along the drawn line through both thicknesses of paper and then opens the sheet to reveal a whole valentine.

3. The valentines are then cut apart into five[1] irregularly shaped, puzzle-like pieces.

4. Instruct the students how to play the game as follows:

A. The object of the game is to be the first player to successfully arrange all of his puzzle pieces into a complete valentine.

B. To begin, each player places one of his valentine pieces on the table in front of him.

C. The player selected to start the game then rolls a die and must call out the name of a musical instrument that contains the *number of syllables* indicated by the number of dots on top of the die when it comes to rest. For example, if a "two" is rolled, the player may respond with "trumpet," "organ," or "banjo."

D. The player must call out his answer before the remaining players complete the spelling of the word M-U-S-I-C in a steady, rhythmic chant.

E. If a player provides a correct answer within the allotted time, he earns the opportunity to place another valentine piece into the puzzle before him.

F. If he does not provide a correct answer or fails to respond within the given time, the player may not add on to his puzzle, thereby losing that turn; play resumes with the roll of the die by the next student.

G. If a "six" is rolled on the die, the player must *remove* a piece from his puzzle; if he has only one puzzle piece before him when a "six" is rolled, he must remove that piece from the playing area and roll a "one" on the die before replacing the initial piece and resuming play.

5. To ensure that each player has the same amount of time in which to call out his answer, you or a selected student may lead the chanting of the word M-U-S-I-C until the players are able to do so by themselves. (The moment that the number appears on top of the die, the students are to begin chanting as the player begins contemplating his answer.)

6. In preparation for the game and to facilitate play, you may ask the students to name various instruments which you list on the chalkboard. Musical instrument names that are acceptable re-

---

[1]Depending on the degree of complexity desired, the teacher may require the students to cut their valentines into *more* than five pieces.

sponses for each number (excluding "six") on the die include the following:

One Syllable

Harp
Gong
Chimes
Flute
Bells
Drum
Horn
Lyre
Lute
Sticks
Jug

Two Syllables

Whistle
Woodblock
Tom-tom
Tone block
Tone bells
Cornet
Oboe
Guitar
Snare drum
Trumpet
Banjo
French horn
Songflute
Rattles
Bugle
Zither
Bassoon
Cello
Trombone
Organ
Sandblocks
Song bells
String bass
Tuba

Bass drum
Cymbals
Claves
Guiro
Hand drum
Bongos

Three Syllables

Vibraphone
Glockenspiel
Harpsichord
Jinglestick
Jingleclogs
Jingle bells
Kettledrum
Piano
Sousaphone
Marimba
Clarinet
Piccolo
Bongo drums
Celesta
Tympani
Maracas
Violin
Viola
Mandolin
Recorder
Tambourine
Xylophone
Triangle
Saxophone
Alto horn
Castanets
Conga drum
Carillon
English horn
Dulcimer

Flugelhorn

Rhythm sticks

Finger cymbals

Melodica

Bass clarinet

Herald trumpet

Four Syllables

Harmonica

Baritone horn

Accordion

Ukulele

Calliope

Euphonium

Five Syllables

Alto saxophone

Alto clarinet

Tenor saxophone

Mellophonium

Resonator bells

STEP - SKIP HEARTS

Game

Objective: To develop the ability to distinguish between musical "steps" and "skips."

Grades: 3 – 6 (entire class participation)

1. Prepare four red felt valentine shapes which may be attached to a flannelboard.

2. Explain to the students the meaning of musical "steps" and "skips"—a step is the distance between two notes that are *close together* in pitch; a skip is the distance between two notes that are *farther apart* in pitch. (For example, on the piano keyboard, two adjoining keys constitute a *step*; two notes that are six keys apart constitute a *skip*. In a set of tone bells, the distance between the bells labeled C and D is a *step*; the distance between C and G is a *skip*.)

3. Play several examples of steps and skips for the students to identify *by listening to the two tones played*. Explain, too, that steps and skips can be represented visually and illustrate them on the chalkboard as shown:

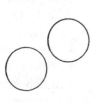

Step

Skip

4. When the students appear to be fairly proficient at distinguishing between steps and skips, divide the class into two teams.

5. Instruct the students how to play the game as follows:

   A. Send one member of each team to the flannel board (which is divided in half by a line); give each contestant two of the prepared felt valentines.

   B. When you play two notes on the piano or tone bells, the contestants are to determine whether the sounds played are representative of a step or a skip.

   C. If a step is played, each student is to arrange his two valentines on his half of the flannel board so that they are *close together*:

   D. If a skip is played, each contestant must place his two hearts on the board so that they are *far apart*:

   E. The first student to accurately portray the step or skip earns a team point.

6. The team that earns the most points is declared to be the winner of the game.

7. To avoid confusion and to facilitate play, make certain that the skips you play are *at least five notes apart*; smaller intervals may be mistaken for steps by the students.

VALENTINE BOX NOTES

Game

Objective: To develop the ability to recognize various musical notes.

Grades: 1 – 3 (class participation)

1. Draw the following musical notes and their names on the chalkboard; pronounce each name and allow the notes and terms to remain on the board for a few days until the students become familiar with them:

   𝄾   – whole note

   𝅗𝅥   – half note

   ♩   – quarter note

   ♪   – eighth note

2. Construct the equipment needed for the activity:

   A. Making the *tactile cards*
      1. From a sheet of sandpaper, cut out one of each musical note listed above.
      2. Glue each sandpaper note securely onto a 3″ × 5″ piece of cardboard as shown:

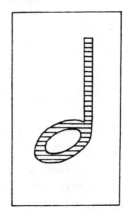

B. Making the *game box*:
Remove the lid from a large shoebox and decorate the sides of the box with colorful valentines, Cupid figures, arrows, lace, etc.

3. Place all four tactile cards into the valentine box and divide the class into two teams.

4. Instruct the students how to play the game as follows:

A. Invite the first member of one team to approach the prepared Valentine box which you hold slightly above the student's line of vision.

B. With both hands, he reaches into the box and takes hold of one of the tactile cards.

C. *Without looking at the card or removing it from the box*, the student runs his fingers over the sandpaper surface of the note; he must identify that note by calling out its proper name.

D. If the student names the note correctly, one point is awarded to his team; if he answers incorrectly or fails to respond within a reasonable amount of time, the first member of the other team is given the opportunity to take a turn at the game.

E. Shake the box to shuffle the cards as the next student approaches to identify a note.

5. The game proceeds as described above until every member of both teams has been given the opportunity to correctly identify a note; the team that earns the most points is declared to be the winner of the game. (In case of a tie, play may be continued until one team errs, thereby causing the game to be won by the opposing team.)

MUSICAL VALENTINES

Project

Objective: To develop familiarity with various musical words and symbols.

Grades: 4 – 6

1. Give each member of the class a pencil, scissors, crayons and/or colored pencils, and one large sheet of red or pink construction paper.

2. Each student folds his sheet of construction paper into quarters; he then draws half a valentine shape on the folded paper as shown:

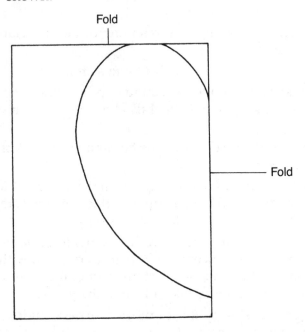

3. The student cuts out the shape through all thicknesses of paper; he then opens and refolds the cutout to reveal a double heart shape which is hinged at the top as illustrated:

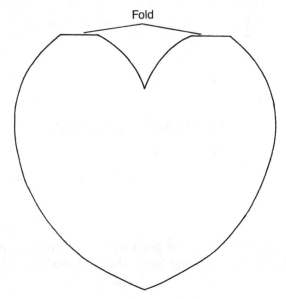

4. Place the following musical symbols and their names on the chalkboard:

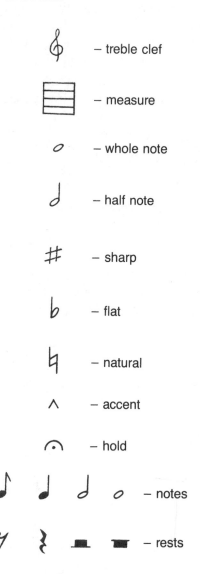

— treble clef

— measure

— whole note

— half note

— sharp

— flat

— natural

— accent

— hold

— notes

— rests

5. Pronounce each term and guide the class in devising appropriate Valentine's Day greetings incorporating the above musical words; list the sample greetings on the chalkboard. For example:

"I won't *rest* until you're my valentine."

"You have my *whole* heart, valentine."

"Valentine, I can't *measure* how much you mean to me."

6. Each student then selects one of the above musical symbol-word combinations with which to decorate and label his cutout valentine greeting card. On the outside of the valentine, he draws the particular musical *symbol* in various positions and formations to create an attractive design; on the inside, he neatly prints an original greeting using the corresponding musical *word*.

7. If desired, the students may send their musical valentines to one another, or you might display them in a prominent place in the classroom.

MUSICAL MOBILE

Project

Objective: To develop familiarity with various words that pertain to the subject of music.

Grades: 3 – 5

1. Give each member of the class two 12" red or white pipe cleaners, a spool of light-colored thread, scraps of red and pink construction paper, a pencil or fine-line marking pen, cellophane tape, scissors, and a ball of modeling clay.

2. Each student gently bends each of his pipe cleaners into half a valentine shape; he joins the two curved ends to form the top of the heart by twisting them securely together as shown:

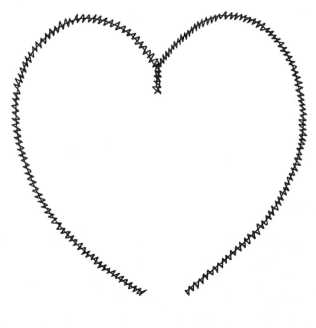

3. The student then flattens one side of the ball of clay which will serve as the base for his mobile. He presses the unattached ends of the pipe cleaners (at the bottom point of the heart) firmly into the clay so that the valentine will stand upright.

4. From the construction paper scraps, the student cuts out five *small* valentines of varying sizes.

5. Each student then selects a five-letter word that is associated with the Valentine's Day holiday—heart, Cupid, arrow, candy, cards, etc.

6. For each letter of his chosen word, the student is to find a word[2] pertaining to the subject of music which begins with that particular letter; for example:

Holiday Word:	C	U	P	I	D
Musical Words:	clarinet	unison	piccolo	instrument	duet
	concert	upbeat	piano	interval	dynamics
	chorus	ukulele	pedal	interlude	drum
	cymbals		pitch		downbeat
	choir		pipe		dot
	castanets		polka		dance
	chimes				
	cornet				
	carol				
	cello				
	clef				
	chord				
	cha-cha				

7. The student then prints *one* letter and *one* word on each of the five paper valentines—a letter on one side and the corresponding word on the other. For example, on the opposite side of the "C" valentine, the word "choir" may be written; on the "U" heart, "ukulele" might be printed, etc.

8. When all five valentines have been labeled on both sides, the student neatly tapes a length of thread to each heart. He then tightly ties the free ends of the thread to the pipe cleaner

---

[2]The students may find it necessary to scan their music texts or books in the school library in order to locate appropriate words.

structure (snipping off any excess thread) so that the valentines are attractively suspended in the proper sequence to spell the holiday word:

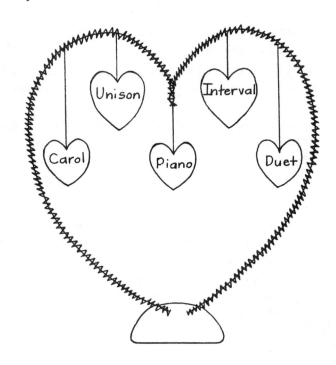

HOP-A-HEART

Rhythmic Activity

Objective: To develop independent rhythmic response to a particular beat using a variety of body movements.

Grades: K – 3

1. Give each member of the class one 90″ length of string. Direct all the students to scatter around the room; each student should stand so he is not touching his neighbor.

2. Tell the students that each of them is to form a valentine shape on the floor with the piece of string.

3. When you begin to play a recording of bouncy, rhythmic music, each student is to step inside his valentine and begin bouncing lightly up and down to the beat; he may engage in additional rhythmic motions, but all movement is to take place within the perimeter of the heart shape.

4. Ring a bell, tap a drum, or produce some other distinctive sound; this is the signal for each student to step over the string border and resume his rhythmic movements *outside* his floor valentine.

5. When you signal a second time, each student hops back inside the valentine and continues his motions.

6. After the class appears to be fairly proficient at alternating their rhythmic movements between the inside and outside of the floor valentines, set various conditions for the students to meet. For example, as you ring the bell, also call out a particular requirement to be added to each student's rhythmic motions. For example, if you announce "Hands on head," the students are to continue bouncing to the music, but they must also place their hands on top of their heads as they move inside and outside the valentines. Additional conditions may include the following:

Right hand on head
Left hand on head
Both hands behind back
Both arms outstretched at sides
Right hand on left knee
Left hand on right knee

7. Types of recordings suggested for this activity include the following:

Various selections of rhythmic, current popular music

Instrumental recordings for creative movement, motor skills development, and physical fitness

Selections of music for gymnastics, floor exercises, rope jumping, and parachute play

7

ST. PATRICK'S DAY

March 17

Remember when you were six years old and believed in all sorts of magic? Not only the "special" magic of Santa Claus, the Easter Bunny, and the Tooth Fairy, but also the "ordinary" magic of making a wish before blowing out the candles on your birthday cake or trusting completely that your lucky key chain would protect you from every danger? Every March 17, you are given a superb opportunity for commemorating the spirit of childhood magic as you and your class prepare for the observance of St. Patrick's Day. Add a wee bit of music to that holiday theme and watch the real magic of your students' enthusiasm carry the day. Hence, the musical activities of this chapter are designed to motivate your students with images of emerald shamrocks and lucky charms, glistening pots of gold and the rowdy antics of the cunning "little people."

Personified by the legendary leprechaun, the distinctive brand of Irish magic is woven into the fabric of the activities of this chapter. "Tricky Leprechaun," for instance, pits the wiles of a mischievous little elf against the listening skills of the students in a whimsical sound activity. In "Enchanted Musical Notes," another crafty imp takes great delight in casting a spell upon the students' drawings of musical notes, and he also plays his naughty tricks in "Musical Symbols Pranks," a team game in which he slyly hides musical symbols for the class to find. The students themselves become "bewitched" as they alternately bounce to a rhythmic beat and then "freeze" in various "Pixilated Poses," and in "Little People Predicaments," they enter the fantasy world of the leprechauns through interpretative movement. Assume the role of the capricious leprechaun yourself in "Shamrock Shenanigans" as you lead the students in demonstrating the opposite functions of the musical note and rest, and "Pot O' Gold" is a novel, subtle means for promoting the class's interest in composers of music and their famous compositions.

The belief in things magic is contagious, and what better time to celebrate that indomitable, childlike spirit than St. Patrick's Day? Enhance that lively, carefree mood with music by planning a roguish rhythmic activity or prankish pantomime. You and your students will enjoy the "wearing of the green" to the fullest, for "when Irish eyes are smiling," you can be sure that music is playing its magical part.

POT O' GOLD
Bulletin Board Idea

Objective: To develop familiarity with various composers of music and their famous compositions.

Grades: 4 – 6

1. Prepare for this activity by covering the bulletin board with plain background paper.

2. You (or a selected student) design the background as follows:

   A. Using colored markers, paints, or oil-based pastel crayons, draw a *large* kettle in the lower right corner of the bulletin board.

   B. Sketch a rainbow which emanates from a white cloud in the upper left corner of the background and extends into the mouth of the kettle.

3. Prepare enough paper slips for the members of the class. Each slip should be labeled with the name of a particular composer. Place all the composer slips into a box or similar container.

4. Give each student scissors, glue or paste, a pencil or fine-line marking pen, and one sheet of yellow construction paper.

5. Direct the class to proceed as follows:

A. From the yellow construction paper, each student cuts out a large disc to serve as a "gold coin."

B. He then withdraws one of the prepared slips from the box and neatly prints the name of the composer at the top of his coin.

C. In addition, the student is assigned the task of locating his particular composer's nationality and one of that composer's famous musical works. (A bit of time spent in the school library will undoubtedly be necessary in order that the students may gather the required information.) The composer's country of birth and the title of his composition are written near the lower edge of the coin. A fully labeled composer coin is shown here:

D. In the space remaining on his coin, the student is to sketch the face of the composer. (If he is unable to find a picture or photograph on which to model his drawing, the student may sketch the composer according to his own imagination.)

6. When all of the composer coins have been designed, invite the class to appropriately arrange them on the bulletin board. In groups of two or three at a time, the students attach their gold coins in and around the kettle in attractive overlapping fashion to suggest the legendary "pot of gold at the end of the rainbow."

7. Names of musical composers suggested for use in this activity include the following:

J. S. Bach	Dvorak	Offenbach
Handel	Grieg	J. Strauss
Haydn	Rimsky-Korsakov	Borodin
Mozart	Ravel	Brahms
Beethoven	Stravinsky	Sousa
Schubert	Prokofiev	Berlin
Rossini	Grofé	Herbert
Mendelssohn	Foster	Rodgers
Chopin	Berlioz	Ellington
Schumann	Puccini	Loewe
Liszt	Debussy	Rachmaninoff
Verdi	R. Strauss	Bartók
Mussorgsky	Sibelius	Ives
Saint-Saëns	Gershwin	Khatchaturian
Bizet	Copland	Varèse
Tchaikovsky	Wagner	Kabalevsky

MUSICAL SYMBOLS PRANKS

Game

Objective: To develop the sight recognition of familiar musical symbols.

Grades: 3 – 6 (entire class participation)

1. On the chalkboard, draw the following musical symbols and their names; allow the symbols and terms to remain on the board for a few days until the students become familiar with them:

    x   – treble clef

    𝄢   – bass clef

    𝅝   – whole note

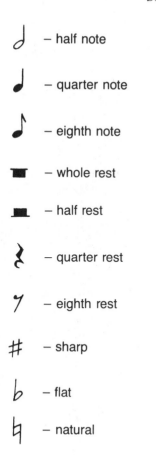

♩ – half note

♩ – quarter note

♪ – eighth note

■ – whole rest

■ – half rest

𝄽 – quarter rest

𝄾 – eighth rest

♯ – sharp

♭ – flat

♮ – natural

⌢ – bird's eye (fermata)

2. Prepare the game cards as follows:

  A. From oaktag, posterboard, or heavy drawing paper, cut several 8½″ × 11″ cards. Draw *four* symbols on each card—*one* of the above musical symbols and *three* non-musical symbols (such as punctuation marks, mathematical signs, etc.).

  B. The four symbols are numbered (with a contrasting colored crayon or marking pen) as shown:

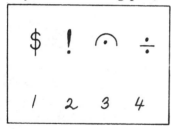

3. Divide the students into two teams; each team line faces you. Hold the prepared game cards so that the symbols cannot be seen by the students.

4. Display the face of one of the cards to the first member of one team; that student must correctly call out the number of the *musical symbol* hidden among the non-musical symbols. For example, on the sample game card illustrated in Step 2, the student must respond by calling out the number "three" in order to accurately identify the musical symbol; he is required to announce the correct number before you slowly count aloud, "one, two, three."

5. If the student correctly names the number of the musical symbol, one point is awarded to his team; if he answers incorrectly or fails to respond within the allotted time, the first member of the other team is given the opportunity to identify the musical symbol. The team that earns the most points is declared to be the winner of the game. (In case of a tie, play may be continued until one team errs, thereby causing the game to be won by the opposing team.)

TRICKY LEPRECHAUN

Game

Objective: To develop the ability to listen for a particular sound.

Grades: K – 2 (entire class participation)

1. Direct the students to form a large circle; each student should stand so he is not touching his neighbor.

2. Blindfold one student and have him stand in the center of the circle.

3. Select a student in the circle to act as the "leprechaun" who is given a tone bell and mallet, a pair of rhythm sticks, or a similar sound-producing device.

4. Upon your signal, the leprechaun begins ringing the bell with the mallet in a definite, steady rhythm.

5. With his arms stretched out in front of him, the blindfolded student slowly walks toward the sound produced by the leprechaun *whom he is required to touch.*

6. After he has successfully reached and touched the leprechaun, the student removes the blindfold and assumes the leprechaun's

position in the circle; the student who served as the leprechaun then moves to the center of the circle and puts on the blindfold.

7. Give the bell and mallet to another leprechaun, and the activity proceeds as described above.

8. Variations of this activity include the following:

   A. As the leprechaun rings the bell, the other students in the circle may simultaneously make various animal sounds to confuse the student in the center; the blindfolded student must then sort through the myriad of sounds and walk only toward the bell-ringing of the leprechaun.

   B. The student who is blindfolded might be seated in a chair as the leprechaun rings the bell in front of the student, behind him, on his right side, on his left side, or underneath him; the blindfolded student must correctly identify the location of the sound.

ENCHANTED MUSICAL NOTES

Project

Objective: To develop familiarity with various musical notes.

Grades: 3 – 6

1. Give each student crayons and/or colored pencils and one large sheet of drawing paper.

2. Place the following musical notes and their names on the chalkboard:

   𝅝 – whole note

   𝅗𝅥 – half note

   𝅘𝅥 – quarter note

   𝅘𝅥𝅮 – eighth note

3. In a second list on the board, write the following adjectives:

> Fat
> Skinny
> Happy
> Sad
> Nervous
> Sleepy
> Angry
> Confused

4. Comment that the musical notes listed above will be "enchanted" (ostensibly by a mischievous Irish leprechaun); direct the class to proceed as follows:

   A. Each student folds his sheet of drawing paper into eight sections; at the bottom of each section, he prints one of the above adjectives.

   B. In random fashion, he then assigns each musical note to a particular adjective and draws the note accordingly. For example, if a student chooses to correlate "fat" with "quarter note," he is then to illustrate his interpretation of a "fat quarter note" in the appropriate section of the paper; a "sleepy whole note" or an "angry eighth note" might follow in the next section.

5. When all eight sections have been illustrated (each note is to be drawn in *two* different styles), the students compare their enchanted musical notes with one another. Display the drawings in a prominent place in the classroom.

PIXILATED POSES

Rhythmic Activity

Objective: To develop the rhythmic response to a particular beat using a variety of body movements.

Grades: 1 – 4

1. Prepare enough construction paper sheets for the members of the class; draw one of the stick figures on page 129 (or figures of your own design) fairly large on each.

2. Arrange the prepared sheets on the floor in a large circle, and attach them securely to the floor with strips of masking tape.

3. Direct the students to position themselves around the outside of the circle of figure sheets.

4. Explain that, as you play a recording of bouncy, rhythmic music, the students are to walk around the circle of figure sheets to the beat and make up their own original patterns of body motions—finger-snapping, hand-clapping, thigh-slapping, or combinations of movements.

5. When you abruptly turn down the volume of the recording, each student is to stop his motions, hop onto the sheet nearest to him, and strike the pose illustrated on the sheet. The humorous result is a noisy, giggling circle of students attempting to assume the various body positions.

6. Turn up the volume and the activity continues until each student has been given the opportunity to strike several poses.

7. Types of recordings suggested for this activity include the following:

Selected bouncy, lively holiday music - e.g., *The Irish Washerwoman, Donegal Round, Fairy Reel*

Various selections of rhythmic, current popular music

Instrumental recordings for creative movement, motor skills development, and physical fitness

Selections of music for gymnastics, floor exercises, rope jumping, and parachute play

SHAMROCK SHENANIGANS
Rhythmic Activity

Objective: To develop independent rhythmic response to a particular beat using a variety of body movements.

Grades: K – 3

1. Enlarge the following, and, using it as a pattern, cut out two shamrocks from green construction paper:

2. On one shamrock, draw a large ♩ ; on the other, a large 𝄽 .

3. Explain to the class that the ♩ is called a musical "note" and that

   the 𝄽 is a musical "rest." Tell the students that each symbol will serve as the signal for them to respond in a particular manner for this activity.

4. Direct the students to scatter around the classroom, and advise them to *keep a close watch on you* for instructions.

5. As you play a recording of bouncy, rhythmic music, the students are to move around the room to the beat, using their own original

patterns of body motions—finger-snapping, hand-clapping, thigh-slapping, or combinations of movements.

6. When you display the shamrock labeled with the *rest* symbol, the students are to abruptly stop their rhythmic movements and "freeze" in place; when you raise the shamrock marked with the *note*, the students resume their motions. Alternately flash the two shamrocks to which the class must correctly react.

7. If a student(s) fails to freeze when the rest is displayed or does not resume his movements when the note is shown, he is declared to be "hexed" and must sit down on the floor for the remainder of that round of play.

8. The activity continues until only one member of the class remains standing; that student then assumes the task of flashing the note and rest shamrocks as the activity begins again.

9. Types of recordings suggested for this activity include the following:

   Selected bouncy, lively holiday music - e.g., *The Irish Washerwoman, Donegal Round, Fairy Reel*

   Various selections of rhythmic, current popular music

   Instrumental recordings for creative movement, motor skills development, and physical fitness

   Selections of music for gymnastics, floor exercises, rope jumping, and parachute play

LITTLE PEOPLE PREDICAMENTS

Pantomime

Objective: To develop the ability to use body movements to describe various imaginary situations.

Grades: K – 3

1. Direct the students to scatter around the classroom.

2. As you play a recording of appropriate music, the students are to pantomime various situations that you announce.

3. The pantomimes are to be descriptive of particular "escape" predicaments in which imaginary "little people" or leprechauns may find themselves. Sample situations for pantomiming include the following:

A. Pretend you are trying to escape from the inside of a mailbox.

B. Pretend you are stuck in a wad of bubble gum.

C. Pretend you are trapped inside a grandfather clock.

D. Pretend you are caught inside a soap bubble.

E. Pretend you have been sealed up inside an envelope.

F. Pretend you have fallen down into a soda pop bottle.

G. Pretend you are trapped inside a birdfeeder.

H. Pretend you are shut up inside a jewelry box.

I. Pretend you have been wrapped up inside a UPS package.

J. Pretend you are caught inside a cookie jar.

K. Pretend you have been closed inside a desk drawer.

L. Pretend you have been zipped up inside your mother's purse.

4. Suitable musical compositions for this activity include the following:

"Londonderry Air" (Irish Tune from County Derry) – traditional

"Dance of the Sugar Plum Fairy" from *The Nutcracker Suite*, Op. 71 – Tchaikovsky

"Dance of the Sylphs" from *La damnation de Faust* (The Damnation of Faust), Op. 24 – Berlioz

Various additional compositions of instrumental music for interpretative movement, pantomime, and ballet

8

EASTER

First Sunday after the first full moon
following the vernal equinox

With diabolical regularity, it strikes every year. It cunningly stalks the innocent and brutally assaults the unsuspecting. Well you know its telltale signs—the restless bodies in perpetual motion; the glassy-eyed staring out of classroom windows; the incessant doodling with pencil and paper; the once attentive thoughts that now drift millions of miles into space. You fearfully recognize those signs as classic symptoms of that annual malady most dreaded by teachers everywhere—SPRING FEVER. Grudgingly, you also admit that the only antidote for that rampant, highly infectious condition is an event known as "Easter vacation." However, with a bit of imagination, the natural appeal of the Easter holiday, and a large dose of music, you can transform your students' spring fever lethargy into exuberant, productive classroom activity.

A familiar symbol of that springtime holiday, the Easter egg, is featured in a number of activities in this particular chapter. "Scrambled Eggs," for example, is a rough-and-tumble team game designed to develop the class's awareness of musical expression words, symbols, composers, and instruments. For learning equivalent musical note values "à la bunny," "Rabbit-in-the-Egg" is a snappy exercise in adding and *multiplying*. Various elements of music are represented in terms of colorful, decorative patterns in "Easter Egg Elements." " 'Opposites Attract' Egg Hunt" offers the students another challenging opportunity for creative interpretation—this time through rhythmic movement. A vocabulary of musical numbers words is explored as the students design the outrageous "Musical Easter Bonnets," and "The Jellybean Shake" is a robust, enjoyable way of introducing contrasting musical rhythms to the students. To commemorate the Jewish springtime festival of Passover, the playful " 'Had Gadya' Finger Puppets" are excellent visual aids for teaching the class a favorite Hebrew folk song. In observance of the arrival of the season itself, "Spring Has Sprung" is an absorbing, educational nature pantomime.

The effective treatment of spring fever in the elementary classroom is quite simple indeed, and, as an enterprising teacher, you need no longer feel defenseless against the attack. Take heart, meet the fever head on, and prepare the proper prescription of musical medicine: Mix equal parts of music and the holiday theme. Shake well and administer once daily at the first sign of distress. Continue treatment until the beginning of Easter vacation. (DO NOT EXCEED RECOMMENDED DOSAGE—Rash of enthusiasm may result!)

EASTER EGG ELEMENTS
Bulletin Board Idea

Objective: To develop an awareness of the various elements of music.

Grades: 3 – 5

1. Prepare for this activity by covering the bulletin board with plain background paper.
2. With a marking pen, print "Musical Easter Eggs" across the top of the background.
3. Select a capable student to draw a *large* Easter basket in the center of the bulletin board with crayons or paints.
4. From several sheets of drawing paper, cut out six large egg shapes; the eggs are to be cut of appropriate size so that they may fit within the basket sketched on the background.
5. Give each member of the class crayons and/or colored pencils.
6. On each egg, the students take turns drawing original decorative

patterns. Each individual design is to represent one of the following "elements" of music (to be listed on the chalkboard):

A. Rhythm = a series of regularly spaced beats—"one, two, three, four; one, two, three, four;" or "one, two, three; one, two, three." Musical examples: "March of the Siamese Children" from *The King and I* – Rodgers; recordings of additional marches (four-beat rhythm). *Tales From the Vienna Woods* – J. Strauss; recordings of additional waltzes (three-beat rhythm).

B. Harmony = more than one sound heard at the same time — multiple sounds. Musical examples: "How Lovely is Thy Dwelling Place" from *German Requiem*, Op. 45 – Brahms. *Russian Easter Overture*, Op. 36 – Rimsky-Korsakov.

C. Expression or Dynamics = louds and softs. Musical examples: Prelude to Act 4 ("Morning") from *Peer Gynt* – Grieg. "Fêtes" (Festivals) from *Three Nocturnes for Orchestra* – Debussy.

D. Melody = the arrangement of pitches in a tune—the "shape" or contour of the line created by connecting the notes of a particular tune. Musical examples: Sonata No. 12 in A-Flat Major, Op. 26, Third Movement – Beethoven (restricted movement between high and low notes within the melody; relatively flat, "passive" melodic line). *For the Beauty of the Earth* – Kocher, Pierpont (considerable movement between high and low notes within the melody; erratic, "active" melodic contour).

E. Tone Color = the quality of musical sound—a large or small group of instruments and/or voices. Musical examples: Symphony No. 1 in B-Flat Major, Op. 38 ("Spring") – Schumann (large group of instruments). Sonata No. 5 in F Major for Violin and Piano, Op. 24 ("Spring") – Beethoven (small group of instruments).

F. Form = the organization of the musical composition, as in poetry—A B A, etc. Musical examples: "To a Water Lily" from *Woodland Sketches*, Op. 51, No. 6 – MacDowell. "Spring Song" from *Songs Without Words*, Op. 62, No. 30 – Mendelssohn.

7. Play a musical example(s) for each individual element; explain the meanings of the above terms while assisting the students in creating representative designs. One small design is to be drawn on every Easter egg by each student until all six eggs are colorfully decorated with appropriate patterns. Sample illustrations include the following:

ELEMENT   **DESIGN AND ITS MEANING**

Rhythm:

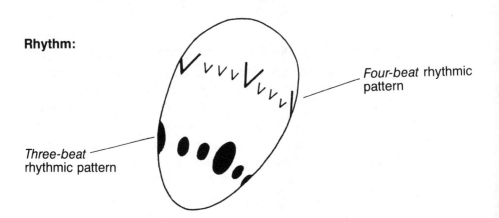

Four-beat rhythmic pattern

Three-beat rhythmic pattern

Harmony:

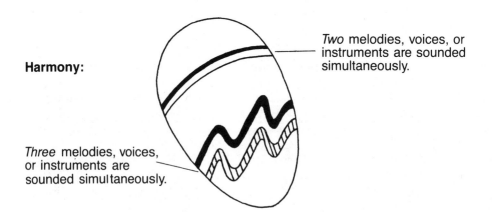

Two melodies, voices, or instruments are sounded simultaneously.

Three melodies, voices, or instruments are sounded simultaneously.

ELEMENT   **DESIGN AND ITS MEANING**

Expression or Dynamics:

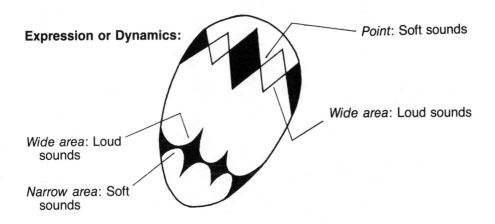

Point: Soft sounds

Wide area: Loud sounds

Wide area: Loud
  sounds

Narrow area: Soft
  sounds

Melody:

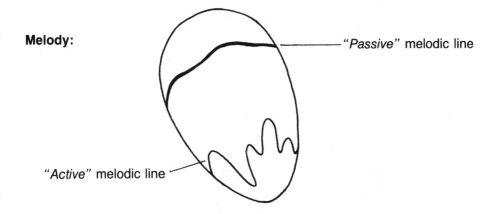

"Passive" melodic line

"Active" melodic line

ELEMENT   **DESIGN AND ITS MEANING**

Tone Color:

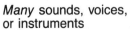

Many sounds, voices, ——
or instruments

————— *Few* sounds, voices, or
instruments

Form (A B A):

Third shape (of the same)
color as the first): The
first melody is sounded
again.

First shape (of a
particular color):
The first melody is
sounded.

Second shape (of a con-
trasting color): A second,
different melody is heard.

8. When all six eggs have been fully decorated, attractively arrange and attach them inside the basket drawn on the bulletin board; over each egg, print the name of the particular element of music.

9. To lend a final holiday touch to the scene, the eggs may be nestled in soft, glossy "Easter grass" which the students might bring from home to line their musical egg basket.

RABBIT-IN-THE-EGG

Game

Objective: To develop familiarity with various musical notes.

Grades: 3 – 5 (two – six players)

1. On the chalkboard, draw the following musical notes; arbitrarily assign a particular numerical value to each and allow the notes and numbers to remain on the board for a few days until the students become familiar with them:

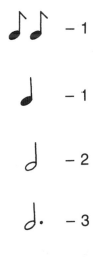

2. Modify six commercially made dice as follows:
   A. Cover each face of every die with a blank self-adhesive label.
   B. On each label, draw one of the above musical note symbols with a fine-line marking pen; on the sixth face of each die, draw a 🐰 .

3. Place all six dice inside a large plastic egg.

4. Instruct the students how to play the game as follows:

   A. The players sit in a circle on the floor. One student, who is selected to be the scorekeeper, is given a sheet of paper and a pencil.

   B. The player chosen to begin the game shakes the plastic egg thoroughly, opens it, and spills the prepared dice onto the floor in front of him.

   C. Using the chalkboard list as a guide, he then adds together the number of points represented by the note values on top of the dice when they come to rest.

   D. If *one* rabbit is rolled among the six dice, the player multiplies his score for that round by two.

   E. If *two* rabbits are rolled, the player loses the total number of points he has earned for that round only.

   F. If *three or more* rabbits are rolled, the player loses all of the points he may have compiled up to that point in the game; he loses his entire game score.

5. After five rounds of play, the student who has amassed the most points is declared to be the winner of the game.

SCRAMBLED EGGS

Game

Objective: To develop familarity with various musical expression words, symbols, composers, and instruments.

Grades: 4 – 6 (entire class participation)

1. Prepare enough oval-shaped "eggs" for *half* the members of the class. Cut them from posterboard or oaktag and label each one with one of the following musical expression words, symbols, composers, or instruments:

Expression Words	Symbols	Composers	Instruments
Allegro	𝄞	Beethoven	Guitar
Largo	𝄢	Debussy	Piccolo
Crescendo	≡	Bach	Trombone
Decrescendo	♯	Saint-Saëns	Marimba
Vivace	♭	Brahms	Violin
Brusco	♮	Mozart	Accordion
Misterioso	𝄐	Tchaikovsky	Chimes
Buffo	∧	Chopin	Saxophone

2. Place all of the prepared eggs face down in an Easter basket and shake the basket lightly to "scramble" the eggs.

3. Divide the students into two teams and line them up at opposite ends of the classroom.

4. Select one team to begin the game; walk down the line of students, each of whom reaches into the basket, withdraws an egg, and holds it face down against his body.

5. Upon a given signal, the team members turn over the prepared eggs and begin "unscrambling" them on the floor, furiously arranging the individual eggs into their proper categories. For example, all of the eggs labeled with the musical symbols are to be grouped together on the floor; the instrument eggs are placed

in a second group, etc., until all of the eggs are divided into the appropriate categories. (Following a considerable amount of noisy excitement, clarification becomes necessary. Thus, when the team members have completed organizing the musical eggs, the students are to *sit down on the floor* in their team line and await your confirmation of their successful accomplishment of the task.)

6. While the team members are engaged in the above activity, record the number of seconds and/or minutes required for the students to unscramble the musical eggs; write the team's time on the chalkboard.

7. Collect the eggs, place them face down in the basket, and scramble them once again. Distribute them to the members of the other team who are given the opportunity to correctly arrange the musical eggs.

8. The team that takes the least amount of time to organize the eggs is declared to be the winner of the game.

9. Depending on the complexity desired or the ability of the particular class, you may prepare a larger number of eggs for the students to unscramble. In addition, several rounds of the game may be played as each team attempts to better its time.

MUSICAL EASTER BONNETS

Project

Objective: To develop familiarity with various musical words that pertain to particular numbers.

Grades: 2 – 6

1. Prepare a spinner for this activity as follows:

   A. Invert a paper plate, and, using a marking pen, divide it into eight sections; puncture a hole in the center of the plate, and label each section with one of the following musical numbers words:

Solo	Quintet
Duet	Sextet
Trio	Septet
Quartet	Octet

   B. From cardboard or oaktag, cut an arrow shape of appropriate size and puncture a hole in the center of the arrow.

C. Line up the two holes, and place the arrow onto the labeled side of the plate; attach the arrow *very loosely* to the plate with a paper fastener (brad) so that it may be spun freely around the disc.

2. On the chalkboard, list the above musical numbers words and their definitions:

   Solo – a composition for or performance by *one* person or instrument

   Duet – a composition for or performance by *two* persons or instruments

   Trio – a composition for or performance by *three* persons or instruments

   Quartet – a composition for or performance by *four* persons or instruments

   Quintet – a composition for or performance by *five* persons or instruments

   Sextet – a composition for or performance by *six* persons or instruments

   Septet – a composition for or performance by *seven* persons or instruments

   Octet – a composition for or performance by *eight* persons or instruments

3. Give each student a pencil, crayons and/or colored pencils, and one large sheet of drawing paper.

4. Tell each student to sketch the outline of a large hat or bonnet on the drawing paper.

5. Have each student, one at a time, activate the prepared spinner and write the musical numbers word he has spun on the reverse side of the sheet of paper.

6. The student then completes his Easter bonnet according to the meaning of his particular musical word. For example, if he spins the word "quintet," the student is to decorate his bonnet with *five* holiday objects—a bright garland of *five* spring flowers, a nest of *five* furry bunnies, a basket of *five* yellow chicks hatching from *five* colored eggs, etc. (The sillier and more outlandish the drawings, the better.)

7. When all of the drawings have been finished, a guessing game may ensue as the class members take turns determining which musical numbers word was spun by each student by counting the Easter decorations on the bonnets.

"HAD GADYA" FINGER PUPPETS

Project

Objective: To develop familiarity with a particular holiday song.

Grades: 2 – 4

1. Enlarge the following pattern; make copies of it and distribute one to every member of the class:

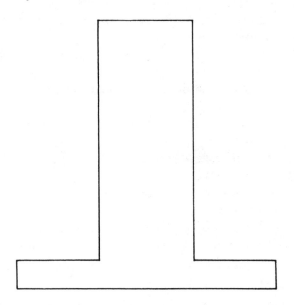

2. Give each student a pencil, crayons and/or colored pencils, scissors, cellophane tape, and one large sheet of heavy drawing paper.

3. On the chalkboard, write the words[1] of the traditional Passover song, "Had Gadya."[2] Underline the ten principal characters denoted in the lyrics (and define any unfamiliar terms):

Verse 1: One little *goat*.
One little goat.
My father bought
For two zuzim.[3]
One little goat. One little goat.

---

[1]This version of "Had Gadya" has been compiled from several translations of the lyrics. Specific words may vary from source to source.

[2]Had Gadya (häd god'yäh), also Chad Gadya – one little goat.

[3]Zuzim (zo͞oh zim') – ancient Hebrew coins.

Verse 2: Then came the *cat*
And chased the goat
My father bought
For two zuzim.
One little goat. One little goat.

Verse 3: Then came the *dog*
And bit the cat,
That chased the goat
My father bought
For two zuzim.
One little goat. One little goat.

Verse 4: Then came the *stick*
And beat the dog,
That bit the cat,
That chased the goat
My father bought
For two zuzim.
One little goat. One little goat.

Verse 5: Then came the *fire*
And burned the stick,
That beat the dog,
That bit the cat,
That chased the goat
My father bought
For two zuzim.
One little goat. One little goat.

Verse 6: Then came the *water*
And quenched the fire,
That burned the stick,
That beat the dog,
That bit the cat,
That chased the goat
My father bought
For two zuzim.
One little goat. One little goat.

Verse 7: Then came the *ox*
And drank the water,
That quenched the fire,
That burned the stick,
That beat the dog,
That bit the cat,
That chased the goat
My father bought
For two zuzim.
One little goat. One little goat.

Verse 8: Then came the *shohet*[4]
And killed the ox,
That drank the water,
That quenched the fire,
That burned the stick,
That beat the dog,
That bit the cat,
That chased the goat
My father bought
For two zuzim.
One little goat. One little goat.

Verse 9: Then came *death's angel*
And slew the shohet,
That killed the ox,
That drank the water,
That quenched the fire,
That burned the stick,
That beat the dog,
That bit the cat,
That chased the goat
My father bought
For two zuzim.
One little goat. One little goat.

Verse 10: Then came the *Holy One*, praised be He,
And destroyed death's angel,
That slew the shohet,
That killed the ox,
That drank the water,
That quenched the fire,
That burned the stick,
That beat the dog,
That bit the cat,
That chased the goat
My father bought
For two zuzim.
One little goat. One little goat.

---

[4]Shohet (shōh′het) – a ritual slaughterer.

4. Explain to the students the dual meaning of the lyrics of the song: As a folksong, "Had Gadya" describes the misadventures of a little goat purchased by a father for his son; however, the lyrics also recount the plight of the Jewish people (the goat) whose history of trials and captivity is ultimately set aright by the intervention of God (the Holy One).

5. Direct the class to proceed as follows:

   A. Each student carefully cuts out the pattern he received.

   B. Placing the pattern onto the drawing paper, he traces around the form to make ten inverted T-shaped figures.

   C. The student cuts out the T-shapes which will be fashioned into ten finger puppets.

   D. On the wide portion of each T-shape, he then colorfully draws one of the persons, animals, or objects cited in the lyrics of "Had Gadya."

   E. The student securely tapes the tab ends of each of the illustrated T-shapes together to form a ring to fit over each of his fingers. (The size of the original T-shape may be adjusted as necessary—a student with a very small hand might require a shorter, more narrow puppet; a student with a large hand may need a somewhat bigger pattern.)

6. When all ten T-shapes have been fashioned into the various characters, the student fits a puppet snugly over each of his fingers; from the little finger of one hand to the little finger of the other hand, he arranges the puppets in *consecutive order* according to the entrances of the characters in the lyrics of the song.

7. Play a recording of "Had Gadya" (or recite the words of the song to the class). The students activate their puppets by holding up and wiggling each finger as the appropriate character is named in each verse of the lyrics.

8. Depending on the ability of the particular class or the degree of complexity desired, elaborate fabric or papier mâché hand puppets may be constructed by the students for the staging of a group puppet play based on "Had Gadya." For the especially ambitious and enthusiastic class, an original pantomime of the story complete with student-designed character masks and/or costumes is a super holiday project.

THE JELLYBEAN SHAKE
Rhythmic Activity

Objective: To develop the rhythmic response to two contrasting musical beats.

Grades: K – 2

1. In preparation for this activity, gather together the following items:

   A. One hand drum (or similar sound-producing device) and mallet

   B. A small box, margarine container, or plastic egg filled with jellybeans

2. Explain to the students that you will perform two distinct rhythm patterns using the drum; demonstrate the patterns as follows:

   A. Four-beat pattern – *tap*, tap, *tap*, tap; *tap*, tap, *tap*, tap; etc. (The
                       1   2   3   4   1   2   3   4
   first and third beats are clearly accented.)

   B. Three-beat pattern – *tap*, tap, tap; *tap*, tap, tap; etc. (The first
                     1   2   3   1   2   3
   beat is clearly accented.)

3. Inform the class that, as you play each rhythmic pattern, they are to respond appropriately. For example, when you perform the four-beat pattern, the students are to *march* around the classroom; when you abruptly shift to the three-beat pattern, the students are to *skip* to the rhythm.

4. Alternate your tapping between the two rhythmic patterns and the students respond accordingly, avoiding collisions with one another as they move around the room.

5. Then, suddenly stop tapping the drum and loudly shake the container of jellybeans; this is the signal for all the students to cease their marching or skipping and immediately sit down on the floor.

6. The last student to sit down when the jellybeans are rattled is declared to be "out" of the activity. Open the container, offer that student a piece of candy, and direct him to move to one end of the classroom until the activity is finished.

7. The rhythmic movement around the room resumes, and the activity continues as described above until all but one student

have been eliminated; he is declared to be the "Jellybean Champion" and is presented with the container of remaining jellybeans as his reward.

"OPPOSITES ATTRACT" EGG HUNT

Rhythmic Activity

Objective: To develop the ability to use body movements to describe various words.

Grades: 2 – 4

1. Prepare enough colored construction paper "eggs" for the members of the class; label the eggs with *words that are antonyms of one another*:

Forward	Backward
Right	Left
Tall	Short
Fat	Thin
Happy	Sad
Good	Bad
Step	Leap
Throw	Catch
Push	Pull
Hot	Cold
Fast	Slow
Awake	Asleep
Nervous	Calm

2. At a time when the students are out of the classroom, hide the eggs in various places throughout the room.

3. When they return to the room, direct the class to proceed as follows:

   A. Upon a given signal, the students scatter around the classroom in search of the antonym eggs.

   B. When each student has found an egg, he is to read the word written on it and keep the identity of the word secret.

   C. As you play a recording of bouncy, lively music, the student is to rhythmically demonstrate the meaning of the word printed on his egg. For example, if his egg is labeled with the word "tall," the student may bounce around the room to the music on tip-toe with his hands stretched far above his head. *All of the student's motions are to be in accordance with the beat of the rhythmic music.*

D. As each student rhythmically interprets his particular word, he is to glance around the classroom in an effort to locate his "partner"—the student who is demonstrating the word that is the opposite in meaning of his own word.

E. When they have found one another, the student pairs move together and continue their motions side by side, illustrating *opposite* movements according to the *same* rhythmic beat. (In addition, the partners are instructed not to talk with each other as they interpret their words; the students are to communicate the meanings of the words with body movements only.)

4. If desired, you may ask for volunteer student partners to perform their antonyms for the class; a guessing game may then ensue as the students attempt to discover the pair's opposite words by carefully watching the gestures of the partners.

5. Types of recordings suggested for this activity include the following:

Selected bouncy, lively holiday music—e.g., *The Bunny Hop*

Various selections of rhythmic, current popular music

Instrumental recordings for creative movement, motor skills development, and physical fitness

Selections for music for gymnastics, floor exercises, rope jumping, and parachute play

SPRING HAS SPRUNG

Pantomime

Objective: To develop the ability to use body movements to describe various events in nature.

Grades: K – 2

1. Explain to the students that they will be pantomiming familiar springtime occurrences in nature.

2. Assign various members of the class to play the following parts in the nature pantomime:

Sun
Raindrops
Breezes
Butterflies

3. Designate the remaining students as "seeds," and as you play a recording of appropriate music, the class portrays the scenes that you announce. For example:

Springtime Scene	Suggested Pantomime
Buried in the ground, the seeds are dormant after the long, cold winter.	Scattering around the classroom, the seed students curl up on the floor, tucking their heads onto their chests and grasping their knees with their hands.
Gentle rain falls on the rich loam covering the seeds.	The students who are portraying the raindrops run gingerly from seed to seed, wiggling their fingers while moving their arms up, down, and from side to side.
Bright rays of sun shine down on the soil.	The sun student extends his arms high over his head in a large circle; he walks slowly among the seeds, "beaming" down on them.
The spring breezes blow across the warm, damp earth.	With their arms swaying, the students interpreting the wind step lightly among the seeds.
Nourished by the sun and rain, the seeds sprout and begin to grow.	Very, very slowly, the seed students unfold their arms and raise their heads.
The seeds mature into fully grown flowers.	From the floor, the seed students gradually rise to a kneeling position and then to a standing posture, gracefully extending their arms over their heads and stretching as if awakening from a long sleep.

Springtime Scene	Suggested Pantomime
Butterflies flit among the flowers.	Moving their arms in wing-like imitation, the students pantomiming the butterflies dart among the flowers.
The fragrant spring breezes return to softly rustle the flower petals.	The flower students gently bend from side to side and front to back as the students playing the breezes reenter the scene and move among the flowers.

4. The nature pantomime is performed several times as various students take turns interpreting the different roles.

5. Suitable musical compositions for this activity include the following:

Symphony No. 6 in F Major, Op. 68 ("Pastoral") – Beethoven

Le Sacre du printemps (Rite of Spring) – Stravinsky

Nocturne in E-Flat Major, Op. 9, No. 2 – Chopin

Various additional compositions of instrumental music for interpretative movement, pantomime, and ballet

9

PATRIOTIC HOLIDAYS OF THE SCHOOL YEAR

Veterans' Day – November 11
Lincoln's Birthday – February 12
Washington's Birthday – February 22
Memorial Day – May 30

Who cares about the patriotic holidays anyway? A lot of elementary school youngsters certainly don't for obvious reasons. Those drab paper silhouettes of Lincoln and Washington that the students fasten to the bulletin board each February can hardly compare with the ever popular Valentine's Day party. And the irresistible, eerie thrills of Halloween easily surpass the annual class lecture on the significance of Veterans' Day. Posing little threat to the sheer joy of decorating the classroom. Christmas tree, the Memorial Day holiday is deemed relevant by the students only as the last official "day off from school" before the start of summer vacation. This year, however, why not consider a different approach? Include a lively American march tune or a rhythmic folk song in your class's observance of the patriotic holidays and watch what happens. Select a star-spangled musical activity from the chapter that follows and prepare to marvel at your students' sudden burst of interest in those school-year patriotic celebrations.

"Folksong Flag," for instance, is a grand classroom adventure in discovering the rich heritage of American folk music. While they create original commemorative designs for their "Musical Stamp Booklets," the students readily become acquainted with the lyrics of favorite patriotic songs and anthems. An introduction to conventional musical notation, "Yankee Doodle" is a light-hearted game of chance based on the familiar Revolutionary War melody. That uniquely patritoic musical genre—the march—is demonstrated in the zany team game, "Taking Shape," and for promoting the rhythmic marching response to assorted sound signals, "Marching Madness" results in an energetic display of knee-lifting and arm-swinging. The ultimate in marching activities, "Rhythm Instrument Parade" not only presents an opportunity for the students to strut their stuff but also provides the perfect occasion for the construction of some innovative handmade instruments that shake, jingle, clack, and thump.

Whether to commemorate a particular historical event or to celebrate the spirit of national pride, music is a thoroughly reliable and versatile means for inspiring eager student involvement in the patriotic observances. To share is to care, and as the students participate together in the musical experience, the patriotic happenings will assume an exciting new quality. So, strike up the band, and color those holidays a very *musical* red, white, and blue.

FOLKSONG FLAG

Bulletin Board Idea

Objective: To develop familiarity with various American folksongs.

Grades: 3 – 6

1. Prepare for this activity by covering the bulletin board with plain background paper.

2. You (or a selected student) draw a *large* American flag on the background with crayons or paints; include the red and white stripes and the blue field, but omit the fifty stars.

3. Give each student a pencil or fine-line marking pen, scissors, glue or paste, and one sheet of white construction paper.

4. From the construction paper, he is to cut out a star shape(s); each shape is to be cut of appropriate size so that fifty stars may fit within the blue field of the flag.

5. On each star, the student is to neatly print the title of a particular American folksong—a spiritual, dance tune, work song, sea chantey, cowboy song, etc. (The students may find it necessary to scan their music texts or books in the school library in search of the titles or they may use those with which they are already familiar.)

6. When fifty stars have been formed and labeled, the class then completes the bulletin board flag. In groups of two or three at a time, invite the students to attach their folksong stars in the proper arrangement on the blue field of the flag.

7. Sample songs titles for use in this activity include the following:

John Henry
Buffalo Gals
Swing Low, Sweet Chariot
Shortnin' Bread
Red River Valley
Shenandoah
Turkey in the Straw
Home on the Range
I've Been Working on the
    Railroad
Ole Dan Tucker
When Johnny Comes
    Marching Home
Polly Wolly Doodle
Old Black Joe
The Old Gray Mare
Doney Gal
Sweet Betsy From Pike
Sourwood Mountain
Lonesome Valley
Blow Ye Winds
There's a Hole in the Bucket
Li'l 'Liza Jane
Green Grow the Lilacs
Oh! Susanna
Old Texas
Skip to My Lou
On Top of Old Smoky
Streets of Laredo

Camptown Races
Go Tell Aunt Rhodie
Down in the Valley
Billy Boy
Blue-Tail Fly
    (Jimmy Crack Corn)
Chicken Reel
Git Along, Little Dogies
    (Dogie Song)
The Crawdad Hole
Shoo, Fly
Springfield Mountain
Way Down Upon the Swanee
    River (Old Folks at Home)
Erie Canal
When the Saints Go
    Marching In
I Ride an Old Paint
Drill, Ye Tarriers
Sacramento
Dixie
Clementine
Rock Island Line
Lone Star Trail
Cindy
She'll Be Comin' 'Round
    the Mountain
My Old Kentucky Home

YANKEE DOODLE

Game

Objective: To develop familiarity with conventional musical notation.

Grades: 2 – 4 (two – six players)

1. Prepare enough game cards for the number of players. Cut each card from colored construction paper in the shape of a particular holiday object. For example, a hatchet for Washington's Birthday; an eagle or flag for Memorial or Veterans' Day; a stovepipe hat for Lincoln's Birthday; etc.

2. Draw the following unit of musical notation—a measure—on the chalkboard:

3. Inform the class that the above illustration is the first measure of the song "Yankee Doodle," and explain that the object of the game is to draw that measure on each game card according to the numbers rolled on a die.

4. Also place the following lists on the board:

Number Rolled on the Die	Procedure	
1	Draw one	(staff)
2	Draw one	(bar line)
3	Draw one	(treble clef)
4	Draw one	(flat)
5	Draw one	(time signature)
6	Draw one	(eighth note)

5. Then direct the students who will play the game to sit in a circle on the floor. Place a die in the center of the circle, and give each player a pencil and one of the prepared game cards.

6. The student who is selected to begin the game rolls the die. If a "one" appears on top when the die comes to rest, the player may draw a staff on his game card; if he rolls a number other than "one," the student loses that turn, and the next player in the circle rolls the die. *Each player must roll a "one" on the die— a staff—before he may add the remaining elements* (designated on the chalkboard list) *to complete his musical measure.*

7. When the student has indeed drawn the staff on his game card, the bar lines, treble clef, flat, time signature, and eighth notes may be added to the measure in any order that they might be rolled on the die.

8. The first player to draw the complete musical measure on his card and call out "Yankee Doodle" is declared to be the winner of the game.

TAKING SHAPE

Game

Objective: To develop the rhythmic response to the marching beat.

Grades: 2 – 5 (entire class participation)

1. Divide the students into two teams, and have each team select a captain.

2. Direct the students to scatter around the classroom; the team members and captains are to intermingle with their opponents, but each student should stand so he is not touching his neighbor.

3. Play a recording of lively march music, and the students begin marching in different directions around the room, lifting their knees high and swinging their arms to the beat.

4. Abruptly turn down the volume of the recording, and call out a particular number, letter of the alphabet, or geometric shape; this is the signal for the students to respond as follows:

   A. The members of both teams quickly assemble in their respective groups in separate areas of the classroom.

   B. The captain of each team then furiously arranges his students into the figure that was announced. For example, if you call out "two," the captain must position each member of his team in such a manner that the arrangement of the entire group forms that number.

5. The first team to accurately display the announced number, letter, or shape is awarded one game point.

6. Turn up the volume of the recording, and the students move out from their team groups to resume marching around the classroom.

7. The activity continues as you call out additional numbers, letters, and shapes to be formed by the students in order to earn game points; the team that amasses the most points is declared to be the winner of the game.

8. Suitable musical compositions for this activity include the following:

"The Washington Post March"—Sousa

"The Thunderer" – Sousa

"Columbia, the Gem of the Ocean" – à Becket

"Hail to the Chief" – Sanderson

Various additional compositions of American march music

MUSICAL STAMP BOOKLETS

Project

Objective: To develop familiarity with various American patriotic songs.

Grades: 2 – 6

1. Enlarge the following postage stamp illustration on the chalkboard:

2. List the titles of several familiar patriotic songs on the board. For example:

God Bless America
This Land Is Your Land
America, the Beautiful
The Star-Spangled Banner
America (My Country 'Tis of Thee)
This Is My Country

3. Give each student a pencil, crayons and/or colored pencils, six sheets of unlined paper, and one sheet of construction paper.

4. Direct each student to draw a large blank postage stamp on each of the six unlined sheets, using the chalkboard illustration as a model.

5. As you play a vocal recording of each of the above patriotic songs, the student is to create an original "commemorative postage stamp" design to represent the lyrics of each tune. For example, while he listens to "America, the Beautiful," the student may draw a colorful landscape on one of his stamps, featuring golden fields of wheat or rugged purple mountains. In addition, he attractively labels the stamp with the appropriate song title.

6. When all six musical stamps have been completed, the student folds his sheet of construction paper in half, making and decorating a cover for the pages which are stapled into booklet form.

MARCHING MADNESS
Rhythmic Activity

Objective: To develop the rhythmic response to the marching beat.

Grades: K – 3

1. Direct the students to scatter around the classroom; each student should stand so he is not touching his neighbor.

2. Explain to the class that you will produce various sounds; each sound will serve as a signal for the students to perform a particular rhythmic action. For example:

Sound	Corresponding Rhythmic Action
Ring of bell	Swinging their arms and lifting their knees high, the students *march forward* around the room.
Shake of tambourine	The students *march in place*.

Sound	Corresponding Rhythmic Action
Tap of drum	The students *march backward* around the room.
Blast of whistle	The students *march in place while nodding their heads to the beat.*

3. Introduce each sound individually to the class, allowing the students to become familiar with the signals until all of the class members are correctly responding to all four sounds with the corresponding rhythmic motions.

4. Play a recording of lively march music and produce one of the above sounds to which the students react with the appropriate motions. After several moments, signal the class with another sound, and the students adjust their actions accordingly.

5. The activity continues as the students march in various directions around the classroom to the beat of the music, performing the different rhythmic movements in response to each of the sounds.

6. Variations of this activity include the following:

   A. As they march forward around the classroom, the students *change direction* every time you ring a bell, tap a drum, or produce some other distinctive sound; each student individually determines the direction in which he will march when the signal is given. For example, each time the bell is rung, the student may pivot on his heel, veer off at a ninety-degree angle, and continue marching in that direction until the bell is sounded again. If he happens to march up against an immovable object such as a wall, desk, or fellow class member, the student must march in place until the bell rings once more, indicating another change of direction.

   B. The students alternately march *with and without musical accompaniment.* After the students have marched around the classroom for a few moments, turn down the volume of the recording. Attempting to maintain the rhythmic beat established by the music, the students continue their marching without an audible accompaniment. Turn up the recording, and the class members march around the room with music once again.

7. Suitable musical compositions for this activity include the following:

   "Semper Fidelis" – Sousa

   "El Capitan" – Sousa

"When Johnny Comes Marching Home" – Lambert
"You're a Grand Old Flag" – Cohan
Various additional compositions of American march music

RHYTHM INSTRUMENT PARADE
Rhythmic Activity

Objective: To develop the rhythmic response to the marching beat incorporating the use of simple, student-made rhythm instruments.

Grades: 1 – 4

In preparation for this activity, the students must bring from home the various materials necessary for the construction of their rhythm instruments.

1. On the chalkboard, list the following four groups of rhythm instruments (which are classified according to sound); assign a particular color(s) to each type:

> Shakers – red
> Jinglers – white
> Clackers – blue
> Thumpers – red, white, and blue

2. Discuss with the class the various ways in which the above instrument types may be constructed. For example:
   Shakers might be made from margarine containers, baby food or cosmetic jars, plastic eggs, or small paper bags or boxes that are filled with dried rice, peas, beans, buttons, etc. An empty toilet paper tube may be flattened, filled with dried rice, peas, beans, or buttons, and securely taped closed at both ends. Half a dozen metal bottle caps might be placed between two paper plates which are fastened tightly together at the edges with staples, tape, or yarn laces.
   Jinglers may be constructed by attaching several metal buttons or bottle caps to the round tops of wooden clothespins with a nail. A kitchen fork dangling from a string might be struck with a large nail. A handful of metal keys or pop-top tabs may be hung from a string or key chain. Metal thimbles might be placed on the finger tips and tapped together. A large nail or bolt may be suspended from a string and struck with another nail or bolt.

Clackers might be fashioned by sliding several dried round steak bones or empty thread spools onto a wire ring. Two wooden spoons, two dried sparerib bones, or two flat stones may be tapped together.

Thumpers may be made from empty oatmeal boxes or coffee cans with plastic lids which are tapped with the hand or a pencil.

3. Assign each student the task of constructing one of the above instruments (or one of his own invention). Several class members may make the same type of instrument, and depending on the degree of complexity desired, the shakers, jinglers, clackers, and thumpers might be decorated according to the taste and ability of each individual student.

4. As the students work on their rhythm instruments, prepare for your role in the activity by tying colored crepe paper streamers onto four long wooden dowels. Red streamers are tied on the end of one dowel; white streamers on another; blue on the third; a combination of red, white, and blue on the fourth.

5. When all of the rhythm instruments have been constructed and the dowels have been prepared, direct the students to form a line behind you; each student carries his instrument in playing position, and you hold the four dowels.

6. Advise the class to *keep a close watch on you* for instructions and caution them that they are *not yet* to sound their rhythm instruments. Lead the students in a parade around the classroom as a recording of lively march music is played.

7. When the parade of marching students is well under way, you then alternately display the prepared dowels to which the class members must respond appropriately. For example, each time you raise the dowel decorated with the *red* streamers high over your head, the students in possession of the *shakers* play their instruments to the beat of the music; when the red dowel is lowered, the shakers are silenced. Every time the *blue* dowel is shown, the class members carrying the *clackers* perform; they stop playing when that dowel is lowered.

8. For additional fun along the parade route, direct selected instrumental ensembles to play; you might raise two, three, or all four dowels simultaneously, signaling that more than one group of instrumentalists is to perform together.

9. The activity continues as you offer various class members the

opportunity to lead the parade of performing students around the room.

10. Suitable musical compositions for this activity include the following:

"The Stars and Stripes Forever" – Sousa

"King Cotton"– Sousa

"American Patrol" – Meacham

"Yankee Doodle" – traditional

Various additional compositions of American march music

PRONUNCIATION GLOSSARY

Accelerando – ăht chĕh lĕh răhn´ dŏh
Ad libitum – äd lib´ i tūm
Allegro – ăhl lay´ grŏh
Brusco – broo´ skŏh
Buffo – boof´ fŏh
Calmato – kahl mah´ tŏh
Celesta – sĕh les´ tä
Claves – kla´ vays
Coda – kō´ dah
Crescendo – krĕh shen´ dŏh
Decrescendo – day krĕh shen´ dŏh
Fermata – fehr mah´ tah
Fine – fee´ nay
Fortissimo – fohr tees´ see mŏh
Fugue – fyōog
Furioso – foo rē oh´ sŏh
Glissando – glee sahn´ dŏh
Grandioso – grăhn dē oh´ sŏh
Guiro – gwē´ rō
Largo – lar´ gŏh
Legato – lĕh gah´ tŏh
Misterioso – mē stĕh rē oh´ sŏh
Pizzicato – pee tsee kah´ tŏh
Poco – pō´ kŏh
Presto – prâ´ stŏh

Ritardando – rē tar dăhn′ dŏh
Staccato – stăhk kah′ tŏh
Subito – soo′ bee tŏh
Toccata – tŏhk kah′ tah
Vivace – vē vah′ chĕh

BIBLIOGRAPHY

Becker, Joyce. *Jewish Holiday Crafts*. New York: Bonim Books, 1977.

Bramscher, Cynthia S. *Treasury of Musical Motivators for the Elementary Classroom*. West Nyack: Parker Publishing Company, Inc., 1979.

Harrison, F. and Westrup, J. A. *The New College Encyclopedia of Music*. New York: W. W. Norton and Company, 1960.

Hirsh, Marilyn. *One Little Goat: A Passover Song*. New York: Holiday House, 1979.

Machlis, Joseph. *The Enjoyment of Music*. New York: W. W. Norton and Company, 1970.

Miller, William Hugh. *Introduction to Music Appreciation*. Philadelphia: Chilton Book Company, 1970.

Purdy, Susan. *Festivals for You to Celebrate*. Philadelphia: J. B. Lippincott Company, 1969.

Schroeder, Ira. *Listener's Handbook*. Ames: Iowa State University Press, 1966.

Index